GOD IS A QUESTION, NOT AN ANSWER

GOD IS A QUESTION, NOT AN ANSWER

Finding Common Ground
in Our Uncertainty

WILLIAM IRWIN

ROWMAN & LITTLEFIELD
Lanham • Boulder • New York • London

Published by Rowman & Littlefield
An imprint of The Rowman & Littlefield Publishing Group, Inc.
4501 Forbes Boulevard, Suite 200, Lanham, Maryland 20706
www.rowman.com

6 Tinworth Street, London SE11 5AL

Distributed by NATIONAL BOOK NETWORK

British Library Cataloguing in Publication Information Available

Library of Congress Cataloging-in-Publication Data

Names: Irwin, William, 1970– author.
Title: God is a question, not an answer : finding common ground in our
uncertainty / William Irwin.
Description: Lanham : Rowman & Littlefield, [2019] | Includes
bibliographical references and index.
Identifiers: LCCN 2018007729 (print) | LCCN 2018042386 (ebook) | ISBN
9781538115893 (electronic) | ISBN 9781538115886 (cloth : alk. paper)
Subjects: LCSH: God. | God—Proof. | Faith.
Classification: LCC BL473 (ebook) | LCC BL473 .I79 2019 (print) | DDC
211—dc23
LC record available at https://lccn.loc.gov/2018007729

∞™ The paper used in this publication meets the minimum requirements of
American National Standard for Information Sciences—Permanence of Paper
for Printed Library Materials, ANSI/NISO Z39.48-1992.

Printed in the United States of America

CONTENTS

ACKNOWLEDGMENTS

This book began when John Loudon suggested that I should write a response to the many readers who commented on my *New York Times* article "God Is a Question, Not an Answer." I thank John for the suggestion, the readers for their comments, and the *New York Times* for permission to reprint part of the article as well as part of another article, "How to Live a Lie." Additionally, I thank Masahiro Morioka, editor of the *Journal of Philosophy of Life*, for permission to reprint part of a previously published article in chapter 7, and I thank Stephen Law, editor of *Think*, and Cambridge University Press for permission to reprint part of a previously published article in chapter 1.

I benefited greatly from thoughtful feedback on earlier drafts of the book manuscript from a wide range of readers including religious believers, atheists, and agnostics: Jim Ambury, Greg Bassham, Eric Bronson, Kyle Johnson, John Loudon, Chris Stine, and Justin Vacula. Allow me to apologize here for not doing a better job of following their advice.

In addition to those who read the manuscript, I was buoyed by support from Dominic Erdozain, Jorge Gracia, Tom Morris, Mark White, and especially my wife, Megan Lloyd. Sarah Stanton, Jon Sisk, Natalie Mandziuk, Michael Tan, Jehanne Schweitzer, and Carli Hansen at Rowman & Littlefield have been a joy to work with, enthusiastic and consummately professional. Sarah Zink's excellent copyediting saved me from some potentially embarrassing mistakes.

In closing, I thank all the people with whom I have discussed God through the years and who have put up with my changing views filled with certainty and uncertainty. Thanks in advance to all readers of this book. I look forward to hearing from you.

GENESIS

Uncertainly Yours

"God Is a Question, Not an Answer." That is the title of an article I published in the *New York Times* on Easter Sunday 2016. It is also the title of the book you hold in your hands. The line comes from *The Meursault Investigation*, a novel that tells the story of Harun, the brother of the unnamed Arab who was killed in *The Stranger*, the classic existentialist novel by Albert Camus. Near the end of *The Meursault Investigation* an imam hounds Harun, and Harun gives a litany of his personal impieties, culminating in the blasphemous declaration that "God is a question, not an answer."[1] Harun's poetic musing resonates with me as a teacher and student of philosophy. The question is permanent, answers are temporary. I live in the question.

Of course, God is not literally a question. Rather, the topic of God raises a question, indeed many questions, the most fundamental of which is: Does God exist? I wrote the article, as I write this book, from the perspective of an "honest atheist," by which I mean one who has doubts. Just as there can be no absolute certainty for the honest religious believer, so too there can be no absolute certainty for the honest atheist.[2]

When I submitted my article to the *New York Times* for consideration, I did not imagine that it would be published on Easter. Because I submitted the piece to the *Times* philosophy blog, *The Stone*,

I did not even think it would be published in the print version of the newspaper. So, when the editors told me it was accepted and would be published in print on Easter Sunday, I had mixed feelings. On the one hand I was elated and grateful for the opportunity, but on the other hand I was apprehensive because Easter is the most sacred day on the Christian calendar, and many of my friends and family members are Christians. They didn't need to hear from an atheist, honest or otherwise, on Easter. To my surprise and delight, I received a number of supportive e-mails from Christians, including priests and ministers. I was prepared for an onslaught of ignorance and condemnation from believers, but I got only a peppering.

The response to the article was remarkable even by the standards of the *New York Times*, with nearly 2,500 online comments. To my dismay, the majority of the comments came from atheists, many of whom were insulted by my suggestion that an honest atheist must sometimes experience doubt. As the comments poured in over the next week, some of them accused me of being a covert Christian who was trying to tell atheists what it means to be an atheist. I wondered how I could be so poorly understood, and I came to realize that it was partly a matter of the format. A short article provides little space to pause and carefully define all the terms, especially weighty ones like "God" and "doubt." Many people were misunderstanding what I meant by "God" and "doubt," and some were misinterpreting me uncharitably.

Experience has taught me that responding online to comments on my articles is unproductive. The forum is just not conducive to the thoughtful exchange of ideas, so I refrained, as usual, from jumping into the discussion online. As I reflected on all the comments, though, it became clear that I needed to say more. The goal of my article had been to find common ground for believers and nonbelievers by focusing on their shared uncertainty. To that extent, the article failed. In other ways, though, it succeeded. The article provoked a reaction among readers, and it made me realize that I needed to write more to clarify my views. The result is this small book on a big topic.

Chapter 1 begins with the central issue of doubt, articulating what I mean by "doubt" and making clear why we all exist in a state of doubt even when we do not realize it. The natural inclination for many people is to try to resolve and dispel doubt as quickly as it arises, but chapter 2 presents a different approach, suggesting that there is value in embracing doubt and even cultivating it. Many people have ruled out the possibility of a particular conception of God, perhaps the one they were raised with or perhaps the one they associate with a certain brand of religion. Chapter 3 considers the variety of conceptions of God, not all of which can be automatically discarded. Short of fully discarding the divine, religious fictionalism poses a novel approach: accepting God without believing God actually exists. Chapter 4 considers and rejects this possibility, religious fictionalism, in which a person treats God as akin to a fictional character in a movie or novel.

Faith is a point of conflict in nearly any discussion of God. If faith is simply belief against evidence, and if the evidence for God is lacking, then faith in God seems foolish or irrational. Chapter 5 explores an alternative conception of faith according to which faith is not chiefly about belief but rather about insight and commitment. Chapter 6 turns to the task of coexistence, suggesting that civil discourse is possible between those who disagree about the existence of God. Indeed, there is much to be learned from one another. Chapter 7 considers a surprising proposal for what atheists can learn and appropriate from believers: prayer. Much as meditation can be practiced with benefit apart from belief in God, so too can prayer. Such prayer is an individual matter, though, and this leads to the caution of chapter 8: beware of secular religions. In light of the preceding chapters, chapter 9 offers personal reflections on my journey thus far.

Clearly, this book is not meant to be the final word on God. It's not even meant to be my final word on God. Rather, it is my attempt to continue living in the question and to encourage the reader to do likewise.

1

YOU CAN DOUBT ANYTHING,
AND YOU SHOULD

In *Meditations on First Philosophy*, René Descartes launched modern philosophy on a quest for certainty, employing a method of doubt. He decided to suspend belief in anything that could possibly be doubted while looking for a piece of foundational certainty, something that could not possibly be doubted. Upon consideration, he found that beliefs based on the senses could be doubted because in the past they had sometimes given him bad information. Objects at a distance appear smaller. We think we hear someone call our name, but no one is there. That kind of thing.

Famously, Descartes examined the seemingly certain fact that he was sitting by a fire with paper and pen. This belief appeared immune to doubt, but then he recalled that he had often pictured the same scene and had the same thoughts in his dreams. In fact, it is a common experience in the midst of a dream to ask oneself if it is a dream and conclude that it is not, only to realize later that it was indeed a dream. All beliefs based on the senses are thus subject to the dream argument: it is always possible, no matter how unlikely, that I am dreaming right now.

Descartes had shown that every belief based on the senses is subject to doubt and thus is not certain, no matter how certain one feels about it. One can feel perfectly certain and yet be in a state of uncertainty. This is much like the way one can feel perfectly safe and yet be vulnerable—one is not in a state of safety even though one feels safe.

The senses cannot deliver foundational certainty, but perhaps mathematics could. Descartes, after all, was a great mathematician in addition to being a great philosopher. He noticed that mathematical truths remained the same even in dreams: 2+3=5 and a triangle has three sides whether I am awake and observing the world or asleep and dreaming. Upon further thought, though, Descartes had a creepy realization: an evil demon could be deceiving him about everything. This evil demon could deceive him not only about sensory experience, but even about simple truths of mathematics. Perhaps triangles don't really have three sides; perhaps the evil demon just makes it appear that way. The scenario didn't strike Descartes as likely, but it was possible. Worse, it appeared impossible to disprove.

As a rationalist and a scientist, Descartes did not think it was likely that an evil demon was deceiving him about his entire experience. He did not *feel* uncertainty on this matter, but he recognized that he was in a state of uncertainty. It is tempting to dismiss Descartes's scenario as the product of an earlier age when belief in demons was common. Ironically, though, the issue that Descartes raised with his scenario has actually become more likely in our age. The film *The Matrix* gives us an updated version of the scenario: nearly all of humanity has been enslaved by a malevolent artificial intelligence that has them hooked up to a supercomputer, which creates a false reality called the Matrix. The average human being seems to be living a typical human life, eating, drinking, sleeping, going to work, and helping the landlady carry out her garbage. In actuality, though, that person is immersed in a pink gooey pod and wired into the Matrix. That person is not living in reality, but in virtual reality. This is the premise of the movie, but it is also a genuine possibility that cannot be disproven. Try to prove that you are not in the Matrix right now! You can't. That doesn't mean that you should worry about it. That doesn't mean that you should feel uncertainty. But it does mean that you are in a state of uncertainty. It means that you should at least occasionally think about this and what it means, that most things aren't as certain as they seem or feel.

Given the improbability of the Matrix scenario, though, you might be tempted to conclude that it's not worth a moment more of your time. Yet, the odds that you are in something like the Matrix may be much higher than you think. The philosopher Nick Bostrom has conjectured that the likelihood may be as high as 20 percent.[1] Bostrom considers the possibility of simulations: virtual worlds with conscious beings created by other conscious beings. Think of a primitive simulated world like the video game series *The Sims*. The inhabitants of *The Sims* world are not conscious, are not self-aware. But if technology advances to the point where we can create conscious, self-aware artificial intelligence, then we will be able to create virtual, simulated worlds populated by conscious beings. These beings will not have brains hooked up to supercomputers; they will be computer creations. And yet they will experience their worlds as if they were as real as our world. Only if they take a philosophy class or read a book like this one will they be tempted to wonder whether they are in fact living in the real world.

We may be inclined to feel pity at the thought of such beings, but we may actually be them. Like the Matrix scenario, it is impossible to disprove. But unlike the Matrix scenario it has a disquieting level of possibility. As Bostrom sees it, there are three possible scenarios. The first is that all societies die out before reaching the level of technological sophistication necessary to create virtual worlds populated by conscious beings. The second possibility is that such societies all lose interest in creating such virtual worlds or have strict moral and legal prohibitions against creating them. The third possibility is that we almost certainly are in a simulated virtual world right now. Here's why: if the ability to make simulated virtual worlds populated by conscious beings becomes common, then there will be many more beings in virtual worlds than in the real world. If every person in the real world has the ability to create a virtual world with a billion conscious beings in it, then, if you are a conscious being, the odds of being in the real world are a billion to one.

So, how likely is it that we are in a virtual world right now? That depends on the probabilities we assign to the three possibilities. There is no good way to determine the objective likelihood of the three possibilities. One way of handling such a situation of limited information is to allot an equal probability to each of the three scenarios until and unless new information becomes available that gives us reason to change those estimates. So we could start by saying that the probability of each of the scenarios is one-third, or 33 and 1/3 percent. If we are given reason to think that it may never be possible to create simulated beings who are conscious and believe themselves to be living in the real world, then we would lower that probability. If we think that the likelihood of societies losing interest in creating simulations or successfully banning them is lower than the others, then we would raise the other two probabilities accordingly. No matter what probabilities we ultimately assign, the chances are much higher than we might originally have thought, and much higher than we might wish, that we are living in a simulated world.

Of course, if we are living in a simulated world, that would explain some things. It would explain why there is so-called natural evil in the world. Famine, disease, and earthquakes are present because the world was not created by an all-loving, all-powerful God, but by an imperfect creature in an advanced civilization. This world of ours might be the equivalent of a hobby or a junior high school science project. The creator and maintainer of our virtual world might not be particularly bright or caring. All of this would seem to count against the likelihood of the existence of an all-loving, all-powerful God, but it would not rule out such a God. There could still be an all-loving, all-powerful God who created the real world. If the intelligent creatures in the real world have free will, then all the so-called natural evil in our virtual world would be the result of free actions taken by creatures in the real world. It would not be God's fault; it would result from the free will of creatures, not the actions of the ultimate creator.

So, am I suggesting that we have reason to worry? No. Even though the chances are higher than we might have realized that we are living in a simulated reality, there is nothing much we can do about it. We have reason to doubt that we are living in the real world; we are in a state of uncertainty. But we have no great cause to feel doubt about it. Rather, we have reason to be humble in what we claim to *know* about our world, recognizing that much of what seems most certain is subject to doubt.

What then does it mean to know something? It means more than simply to believe it. Justification settles a disagreement between two beliefs. The justification for believing that the sun is a star is conclusive. By contrast, you may believe there is life after death whereas I do not. There is no evidence or justification to conclusively settle this matter. I may argue that the best evidence suggests we are purely physical beings and thus there is nothing about us that could possibly survive the death of the body. You may argue that the design of the universe and your religious faith lead you to believe that this life is not all there is. Neither of us can provide incontrovertible evidence that our belief is true. There may be better arguments on one side of this issue than the other, but the issue cannot be completely settled.

Knowledge has traditionally been defined as justified, true belief.[2] There is no such thing as false knowledge; knowledge is always rooted in true belief. Because true belief can result from luck or accident, more is required for knowledge, namely justification. If I believe that it will rain tomorrow but I have no good reason—justification or evidence—for believing so, we would not say I know it will rain tomorrow, even if it does rain.

But does any belief really have enough justification behind it to count as knowledge? Not if we require absolute certainty for justification. That "1+1=2" and that "I'm a human being living in the twenty-first century" may seem like the kind of true beliefs so firmly justified that they surely count as knowledge. But it is always at least remotely possible that we (or I, if I am alone in the universe) are the victims of mass deception in a Matrix-like scenario, that even the most fundamental, obvious, and justified things we believe are actually false. For practical purposes, then, we cannot require absolute certainty for justification. As a result, we can know something, but we cannot know that we know it. As the American philosopher William James said, "To *know* is one thing, and to know for certain *that* we know is another."[3]

Truth and justification depend on one another in a way that listing them as separate conditions does not reflect. With truth and justification we rob Peter to pay Paul. Thus, although the truth exists objectively and independently of us, we can never be absolutely certain we grasp it. We may have justification for believing that something is true, but no amount of justification is ever sufficient to absolutely guarantee truth. Even the preceding assertions may not be true, though if anything I believe is true, I would wager they are.

All is not lost for justification and knowledge, however. In general, we are justified in believing that things are (for the most part) as we perceive them, remembering, though, that a shift in perspective may eventually show them to be otherwise. This is not to say that reality is exactly as we perceive it. For example, red is not in the apple but in the perception. Still, the working assumption needs to be that reality is as it appears, until and unless there is good evidence to the contrary.

What, then, is evidence or justification? How much justification and what kind of justification we need for knowledge are matters of scholarly debate. Specifying exactly what counts as relevant is difficult business, but it's usually easy to tell in a particular case whether justification is relevant and sufficient or not—even if we can't fully, clearly articulate the criteria for relevance. Given things as we perceive them, using logic and reason, what follows? Recognizing it is always potentially possible that we are wrong, what seems to be the case? What should we most reasonably and logically believe to be true? We need to believe in accord with evidence.

Being mildly overconfident in our ability and knowledge has the advantage of inclining us to achieve beyond objective expectation, but in general, overestimating our justification is a bad habit. Many beliefs feel as certain as can be: that I am typing this right now, or that you are reading this right now, for example. We acknowledge Matrix-like scenarios as possibilities, but that you are reading this right now is as certain as beliefs get. We do well to acknowledge the remote possibility of hypothetical skeptical scenarios, though we would be foolish to be concerned about them in a way that made us reluctant to act on our beliefs. On the other hand, lots of other beliefs come with far less justification and should be attended with a correspondingly lesser feeling of certainty.

The words "logical" and "rational" are sometimes used synonymously, but there is a difference between logical thinking and rational thinking. For example, logically it may be possible for you to reunite with your former spouse. No formal laws of logic are violated in reaching the conclusion that this is possible; there is no logical contradiction involved. But rational thinking—the use of reason—based on experience, suggests that a successful reunion is highly unlikely. The relationship did not work out in the past, and nothing has truly changed about or between the two of you. It would be logical to conclude that the two of you *could* successfully reunite, but it would not be rational.

Lack of certainty is simply the human condition. Consider the issue of intention in interpretation. For example, we may want to know whether J. K. Rowling really intended for Dumbledore to be gay or if she made that up after having published the *Harry Potter* novels. Whatever conclusion we reach, we have to admit our lack of certainty.[4] The same is true in wondering what your mother really meant when she said that your new romantic interest "seems nice."

Any responsible prediction must be accompanied by a margin of error and a confidence level. There is no absolute certainty in prediction. For example, a pollster cannot predict the outcome of an election with 100 percent certainty. Rather, the pollster will supply a margin of error, and that margin of error will itself be understood to have only a degree of certainty. For example, Smith is predicted to beat Jones by 6 percent, and there is a margin of error of 2 percent. So the prediction is outside the margin of error. However, the margin of error itself comes with a confidence level, usually a 95 percent probability. In other words, the chances are 95 percent that the margin of victory will be within 2 percent of a 6 percent victory. This means that there is a 95 percent chance that Smith will win by a margin of victory somewhere between 4 and 8 percent. There is always the possibility of a "Black Swan," a completely unexpected game-changer.[5] Smith could win by an even greater percentage or he could actually lose. These scenarios are highly unlikely, but they are possible. The election of Donald Trump, despite what nearly all the polls predicted, reinforces this point, and it demonstrates the need for epistemic and intellectual humility.

What is true about the science of predictive polling is true about the human condition in general. Even $2 + 2 = 4$ comes with a confidence level. In this case, the possibility of error is vanishingly small and not ordinarily worth considering. The relevant possibility is that we are living in a simulated reality in which the laws of mathematics are produced for us and are subject to change. The same would be true of the laws of logic, such as the law of noncontradiction.[6]

Socrates said that the unexamined life is not worth living. In part, this means that we should not treat our beliefs as ever so fully settled that they are beyond all doubt and the possibility of reconsideration. We must be ready and willing to give up any belief when sufficient reason to the contrary is given. Sometimes the available evidence is inconclusive in the sense that it is not overwhelmingly in favor of one answer over another, but it's very rarely an exact tie. We must believe with the evidence, not against it. The readiness to abandon a previously held belief takes courage and is the sign of a true philosopher.

Willingness to give up a belief should be made easier by the fact that belief is not an all-or-nothing affair. Even the most fundamental beliefs come with a confidence level of less than 100 percent. The actor Peter Ustinov once said that "Beliefs are what divide people. Doubt unites them."[7] This is a clever reversal of what is usually thought to be the case. Even people who share a set of beliefs tend to have disagreements about those beliefs. So, instead of looking to belief for common bonds with some people that divide us from other people, we can look to what unites us with all people: doubt.

God is haunted by doubt; no one can have 100 percent certainty when it comes to God. Nathaniel Hawthorne said of Herman Melville, "He can neither believe, nor be comfortable in his unbelief; and he is too honest and courageous not to try to do one or the other."[8] Any honest atheist must admit that she has her doubts, that occasionally she thinks she might be wrong, that there could be a God after all—not necessarily the God of the Judeo-Christian tradition, but a God of some kind. Dwelling in a state of doubt, uncertainty, and openness about the existence of God marks an honest approach to the question. There is no easy answer. Indeed, the question may be fundamentally unanswerable.

Some atheists take umbrage at this, claiming that they never have any doubts about their unbelief. As with "God," though, we need to get clear about what we mean by "doubt." Doubt, as I mean it here, is a condition of uncertainty and not necessarily a feeling of uncertainty. As we have seen, Descartes showed that it is possible to doubt the existence of the external world because of the possibility of deception by a malicious demon. Updating that line of thought, Bostrom has argued that the chances that we are living in a computer simulation are substantially higher than we might suspect. Bostrom is not asking us to worry and experience feelings of doubt, but he is pointing to reasons for doubt and showing why we are in a state of uncertainty. Likewise, I am not necessarily asking the atheist to worry about the issue of God the way that Melville did.

Some atheists may object that belief in God is unreasonable, even if strictly speaking it is not illogical when it comes to some conceptions of God. However, epistemic standards are context relative for justification in different times and places. Belief in ghosts is not unreasonable in certain times and places, such that the person who does not believe in ghosts at such times and places should at least wonder and doubt occasionally, admitting that he could be wrong. In contemporary America it is no longer reasonable for scientifically educated adults to believe in ghosts, and so the person who does not believe in ghosts is not obligated to feel doubt or wonder about them. However, in contemporary America many scientifically educated and highly intelligent people do believe in God, and they can offer reasons and arguments for their beliefs. This means that the nonbeliever is obligated to at least wonder whether he is right, to admit uncertainty. This may change with time; God may go the way of ghosts, but it has not happened yet. Some people who have been raised by atheists and among other atheists may be much less inclined to doubt or wonder for more than a passing moment. That's fine and perhaps even good.

To be clear, I am not shifting the burden of proof. Someone who makes an existential claim, i.e., a claim that something exists, has to take on the burden of proof for establishing it. Not all existential claims are as ridiculous or as easily dismissed as others. Someone who makes up a religion on the spot can be easily dismissed. But someone who subscribes to a religion with a long history that claims to have its roots in historical events cannot be as easily dismissed. The burden of proof is still on the believer, but the skeptic owes an open mind and due consideration. It remains the case that we should believe in accord with evidence, but we must recognize that when it comes to God, the evidence, or lack thereof, is not complete. We exist in a state of uncertainty, whether or not we have feelings of doubt. Some will conclude that God's nonexistence is beyond a reasonable doubt, but it cannot be claimed to be without a shadow of a doubt.

Belief occurs along a continuum of certainty, and it can never reach absolute certainty.

God is a question of ultimate importance and cannot simply be treated as if it is fully settled. For the honest atheist, like Jean-Paul Sartre, atheism is "a fragile and never-concluded enterprise."[9] In other words, the atheist's unbelief must constantly renew itself in the face of the challenge that others pose and the temptation to believe. The atheist ought to avoid becoming the person of whom William James quipped, "He believes in No God, and he worships him."[10] Once people become settled on a worldview they tend to become defensive of it. As there is defensive religious belief, so too there is defensive atheism. This seems to occur even when someone has lost or given up a previous worldview, as is the case with most atheists. Rather than adopt an orientation of intellectual humility with regard to their new worldview of atheism, some atheists become defensive of it. This is perfectly natural, though regrettable and misguided. We ought to regularly and open-mindedly reconsider the opposing side of the argument, if only to remind ourselves why we believe what we believe.

2

LIVING WITH DOUBT

Many people are inclined to protect a handful of cherished beliefs, no matter what. But believing things doesn't make them so. For some people, the psychological need to believe overrides all reason and logic. It would be too terrible if, for example, there was no God, or there was no afterlife. Unfortunately, just because something would be too terrible is never a good enough reason for concluding it isn't true. As the philosopher Miguel de Unamuno says, "The disastrous consequences of a doctrine prove at most that the doctrine is disastrous, but not that it is false, for there is no proof that the true is necessarily that which suits us best. The identification of the true and the good is but a pious wish."[1]

Sincerely religious people often struggle with doubt. Indeed, it has been said that there is no faith without doubt. The Jewish tradition is noteworthy for its long history of questioning and doubting God, and the following story is illustrative: "One day the followers of a beloved Hasidic rabbi approached him and, with trepidation, told him that the village nonbeliever was on his way to approach the rabbi in the town square with conclusive proof that God does not exist. Minutes later, the nonbeliever approached the rabbi for this purpose. The rabbi listened carefully, and then said one word to him, after which they both burst into tears and embraced. When his followers asked the rabbi what he had said, he told them that he had said one word in Yiddish to the nonbeliever. What was the word? The word was *ephshar* [*efsher*], Yiddish for 'perhaps.'"[2]

In the Christian tradition, doubting begins with Thomas. Notably, the story of Thomas appears in only one of the four Gospels, the Gospel of John. As the story goes, the risen Jesus had appeared to a roomful of followers who then told Thomas about it. Infamously, Thomas said he would not believe it until he felt the wounds in Jesus's hands and side. Can you blame him? Thomas had no reason to think that Jesus would come back from the dead. Jesus had been a great teacher, but Jesus had not explicitly taught that he himself was God—at most he had hinted at it. Thomas was justified in thinking that his friends were suffering from a collective delusion. According to the Gospel of John (John 20:24–29), when Jesus appeared to the followers again Thomas was among them. Jesus chastened Thomas, saying, "'Put your finger here; see my hands. Reach out your hand and put it into my side. Stop doubting and believe.' Thomas said to him, 'My Lord and my God!' Then Jesus told him, 'Because you have seen me, you have believed; blessed are those who have not seen and yet have believed.'"

This is an unfortunate story, and there is no reason to think it is true unless one takes the Bible literally. If the story were true, the authors of the other three gospels would have reported it as well—it certainly is noteworthy. (Of course, even if all four authors reported it, that alone would not be enough to guarantee the truth of the story.) Even if someone believes that Jesus rose from the dead and appeared to his followers, they should not believe this particular story about Thomas. It is clear that the author of the Gospel of John (the last of the four Gospels to be written, c. 90–110 AD) is chiding his contemporary readers. When the author wrote this text, it had been several generations since the life of Jesus, and the author's readers would have been right to express doubts about the events he describes. But rather than comfort and validate them in their doubt, as would have been appropriate, the evangelist scolds them by implicitly saying, "Don't be a doubting Thomas. Jesus blesses those who have not seen and yet believe." The message is that it is better not to doubt—just believe. But the message is also that doubt can be forgiven. Unfortunately, one enduring legacy of the story has been the ideal of a muscular belief, impervious to doubt.

Thankfully, many leading Christians through the centuries have acknowledged their inability to live up to that ideal, notably Mother Teresa, who struggled with the absence of God in her spiritual life. In 1948 Mother Teresa felt called by God to care for the poor in the slums of India, but for a period of about forty years thereafter she experienced profound doubts concerning God. In her letters she writes, "I have no faith . . . If there be God—please forgive me. . . . In my soul I feel just that terrible pain of loss—of God not wanting me—of God not being God—of God not really existing."[3] Rather than diminish her saintliness, Mother Teresa's doubts only add to it. It is one thing to do the difficult work of caring for the poor when one feels that God is sanctioning it, but it is quite another, more admirable, thing to do that work when one doubts whether there is a God. As John D. Caputo writes, "I like to think that Mother Teresa's finest moments were the doubts she endured, those moments when it came over her that she just might not really believe in God or accept any of the doctrines defined by her Catholic faith. What I am drawn to here is not the sight of a good woman suffering but the fact that she never expressed any doubt at all about her *work*, that her works of love fell free of her doctrinal doubts."[4]

Along similar lines, in *New Seeds of Contemplation*, Trappist monk Thomas Merton says, "You cannot be a man of faith unless you know how to doubt. You cannot believe in God unless you are capable of questioning the authority of prejudice, even though that prejudice might seem to be religious."[5] In addition, Merton says:

> Let no one hope to find in contemplation an escape from conflict, from anguish or from doubt. On the contrary, the deep, inexpressible certitude of the contemplative experience awakens a tragic anguish and opens many questions in the depths of the heart like wounds that cannot stop bleeding. For every gain in deep certitude there is a corresponding growth of superficial "doubt." This doubt is by no means opposed to genuine faith, but it mercilessly examines and questions the spurious "faith" of everyday life, the human faith which is nothing but the passive acceptance of conventional opinion. This false "faith" which is what we often live by and which we even come to confuse with our "religion" is subjected to inexorable questioning. . . . Hence is it clear that genuine contemplation is incompatible with complacency and with smug acceptance of prejudiced opinions. It is not mere passive acquiescence in the *status quo*, as some would like to believe—for this would reduce it to the level of spiritual anesthesia.[6]

The struggle that Merton describes will not appeal to all people. We naturally crave a feeling of certainty, and people routinely overestimate the degree of certainty they are warranted in having in their everyday beliefs. An epistemic admission of uncertainty can lead to an uncomfortable feeling of uncertainty, and some people seem temperamentally disinclined to live with this feeling. The rejection of uncertainty is common among religious fundamentalists, but it is also found among some atheistic fundamentalists. Here we may think of science popularizers like Stephen Hawking, Neil deGrasse Tyson, and Bill Nye, who at times have spoken against the value of philosophy. These scientists are highly curious and capable of abstract thought in one domain, and yet they seem to lack curiosity and abstract thought in another. This is a strange phenomenon because scientists generally recognize that there is no absolute certainty in science and that all theories are subject to revision.

The renowned physicist Richard Feynman, for example, said, "I can live with doubt, and uncertainty, and not knowing. I think it's much more interesting to live not knowing than to have answers which might be wrong. I have approximate answers and possible beliefs and different degrees of certainty about different things."[7] Nonetheless, Feynman insisted on being classified as an atheist rather than an agnostic, saying, "Agnostic for me would be trying to weasel out and sound a little nicer than I am about this."[8] Rather than certainty, science offers degrees of probability, yet many scientists like Feynman view the existence of God as only about as probable as the existence of an undiscovered planet between Earth and Mars. They are mistaken, however, if this is their estimate of the probability of God. As we will see in chapter 3, there are many possible conceptions of God, and some are not easily dismissed. When it comes to God, scientists should take the bolder stance of embracing uncertainty. Just as the admission of uncertainty has value in the scientific realm for yielding results and remaining open to future correction, so too does the admission of uncertainty have value in the philosophical realm for living an authentic life and remaining open to future correction.

In response to my *New York Times* article that forms the basis of this book, Damon Linker wrote,

> [Irwin] assumes that all people are equally capable of engaging in the thought-process that leads away from certainty about God and toward doubt. He also assumes that once this uncertainty is achieved, a person will persist in it going forward through life. This is an egalitarian assumption, and it is flatly untrue. . . . Any effort to get large numbers of people to affirm doubt and uncertainty in matters of religion needs to wrestle with this discouraging and sobering track record. Above all, it needs to confront the fact that skepticism isn't for everyone, or even for more than a few. Most people would prefer to

enjoy the comfort of believing themselves to possess comprehensive answers to the deepest mysteries of human existence than to live with the spiritual turbulence that accompanies a life of continual, open-ended doubt. Which is another way of saying that not everyone is cut out to be a philosopher. That's something that even philosophers themselves sometimes need to be reminded of.[9]

Linker's point is well taken. Of course, cultivating doubt is a bit of a philosopher's luxury and does not suit everyone's temperament. We often have to make decisions and move forward; focusing on lack of certainty can be paralyzing and dangerous. Some people simply don't have the temperament to doubt or live in doubt; not everyone is philosophically inclined. That may be. Not everyone has an aptitude to think mathematically beyond a basic level; not everyone has a propensity to write poetry or play music; and so we have to wonder if some people simply have a low base level of philosophical curiosity.

I would expect atheists as a group to have a higher than average level of philosophical curiosity, and maybe they do. I would expect this because most atheists were not raised as atheists but rather came to their atheism upon reflection. I have encountered a number of individual atheists, though, who seem to lack philosophical curiosity and capacity for abstract reflection on questions of knowledge and reality in terms of doubt and certainty. They may, though, be just a small but vocal minority. By contrast, Jesse Bering, a scientist and an atheist, expresses an appropriate sense of doubt and uncertainty in reflecting on the evolutionary argument against God when he says

Does all of this disprove the existence of God? Of course not. Science speaks only to the improbable, not the impossible. If philosophy rules the day, God can never be ruled out entirely, because one could argue that human cognitive evolution was directly and intentionally inspired by God, so we alone, of all species, can perceive Him (and reality in general) using our naturally evolved theory of mind. But if scientific parsimony prevails, and I think it should, such philosophical positioning becomes embarrassingly like grasping at straws. The facts of the evolutionary case strongly imply that God's existence is rather improbable.[10]

Bering keeps the door cracked open just slightly. He will not lose sleep wondering if there is a God, but neither will he overestimate the degree to which his evidence and arguments count against the existence of God. Bering is what I would call an honest atheist. Just because he admits that the nonexistence of God is not certain, does not make him an agnostic, not unless we classify anyone who admits to any uncertainty as an agnostic—and that would be unhelpful. Bering illustrates that we can live with uncertainty. The condition of uncertainty is unavoidable, and experience of doubt and uncertainty comes in many varieties. It does not need to be, nor am I advocating for, a constant feeling of disorientation, of not knowing what is up and what is down. Rather, as the Buddhist practitioner Stephen Batchelor says, "Doubt in this context does not refer to the kind of wavering indecision in which we get stuck, preventing any positive movement. It means to keep alive the perplexity at the heart of our life, to acknowledge that fundamentally we do not know what is going on, to question whatever arises within us."[11] Indeed, the Zen tradition prizes doubt as the key to awakening. According to a Zen dictum, "Great doubt: great awakening. Little doubt: little awakening. No doubt: no awakening."

For me, this "keep[ing] alive the perplexity at the heart of our life" is what it means to say that God is a question, not an answer. This is what it means to say that when it comes to God, answers are temporary and questions are forever. This is what it means to say that I dwell in the question. Ishmael in *Moby Dick* captures this well when he reflects that through all the thick mists of the dim doubts in my mind, divine intuitions now and then shoot, enkindling my fog with a heavenly ray. And for this I thank God; for all have doubts; many deny; but doubts or denials, few along with them, have intuitions. Doubts of all things earthly, and intuitions of some things heavenly; this combination makes neither believer nor infidel, but makes a man who regards them both with equal eye.[12]

Ishmael's description may not appeal to all people, and all my insistence on doubt and uncertainty may strike some people as a kind of militant or aggressive or dogmatic agnosticism. How could that be any better than dogmatic belief or dogmatic atheism? That is a fair question. It is not my point to say that everyone should admit to the same degree of doubt and uncertainty on the question of God. Nor is it my point to say that everyone should experience that doubt and uncertainty in the same way. My point is simply that, when it comes to God, we will never amass enough evidence or good enough arguments to reach complete certainty.

Indeed, the ancient skeptics seem to unwittingly make this point by their example. Socrates had claimed to know nothing, and Pyrrho the skeptic took Socrates quite literally. Not only do we not know about the gods or the nature of the universe, we don't even know if our senses are giving us reliable information. So it was Pyrrho's practice to respond to all questions and issues by saying "I don't know" or "I suspend judgment." As you might imagine, this caused some practical difficulties. Legend has it that Pyrrho's friends would often have to move him out of the way of oncoming carts and keep him from walking over cliffs because he refused to conclude that he knew those things were in front of him. This makes skepticism sound like a foolish and impractical philosophy. What was the point, then? The goal of Pyrrho and the skeptics was akin to that of the Stoics and the Epicureans: peace of mind, freedom from inner disturbance.

The Stoics aimed to achieve peace of mind by exercising self-control, particularly with regard to the emotions. The Stoic Epictetus argued that it is not things that disturb us but our judgments about things. Emotional upset results from false judgments about the world. For example, it is not someone's words that insult us, but our own judgment about whether those words express some truth. The Stoic wisdom maintains that it is easier to change one's mind than to change the world. Thus Epictetus advised, "*Do not seek* to *have everything* that *happens happen* as *you wish, but wish* for *everything* to *happen* as it actually *does happen,* and *your life will* be *serene.*"[13] Stoicism is therefore a philosophy of acceptance. Peace of mind and freedom from anxiety come from acceptance. Of course, this does not mean that we should become doormats and accept it when people walk all over us.

We can influence people and things in the world; we just can't control them. What we can control, with proper effort and training, is our own minds: our thoughts, feelings, and reactions. People and things outside our minds can only be influenced, and all attempts at influence come at a price. In each case, we must determine for ourselves whether we are willing to pay the price to exercise influence or whether we would be better off simply accepting the matter as it is. For example, no student can control her grade on an exam, but she can influence her grade by studying for the exam. Studying is very likely to result in a better grade, but it is not guaranteed to result in the grade she wants. And studying comes at a price in terms of time and energy that could have been spent on other activities. Experience and wisdom are needed to determine which situations are worth the price of influencing and which situations are better to accept.

The Epicureans took a different path to peace of mind: they cultivated pleasure. In today's English an epicure is roughly synonymous with a gourmet, someone with refined taste in food and drink. But this misrepresents the approach of Epicurus and his followers. Their philosophy was to enjoy simple pleasures taken in moderation, so as to maximize pleasure over the long run of life. Epicurus and his followers weren't prudes, and they did not condemn any pleasures as sinful. Rather, they saw some pleasures as being unnecessary. Any source of pleasure, the absence of which would not result in pain, is an unnecessary pleasure. So, for example, exotic food and fine wine are unnecessary pleasures because not having them will not cause pain. All we need is simple food and water. It's all right to indulge in fancier food and drink if and when it is available, but it isn't necessary. In fact, we need to be on guard against pleasures that are unnatural, those that can never be satisfied no matter how much we have. Here it is easy to think of addiction: the addict can never get enough of whatever he craves. Some people are addicted to drugs, some to alcohol, some to nicotine, some to caffeine, some to sex, gambling, money, shopping . . . the list goes on. For the Epicurean, none of these pleasures would be considered bad in itself, but the craving for them can become unnatural and can return more pain than pleasure. Thus, wisdom needs to guide us in determining which of these things to avoid.

Perhaps the simplest and yet the greatest pleasure is peace of mind, which is not an intense state of bliss, but rather a tranquil state of calm, free from emotional upset. Whereas the Stoics advised exercising control of one's emotional domain to achieve peace of mind, the Epicureans advised the life of simple pleasures taken in moderation. Although the Stoics and Epicureans were rival schools of philosophy in their day, they share much in common, and some people mix and match their parts. Each school seems to have something right about how to achieve peace of mind, even if neither seems to see the whole picture.

Skepticism seems to be the odd man out. It's easy to see how under some circumstances the Stoic approach of emotional self-control will lead to peace of mind, and it's easy to see how under some circumstances the Epicurean approach of moderate pleasure will lead to peace of mind. But how could suspending judgment and saying "I don't know" lead to peace of mind? Well, consider tough decisions with no clear best choice. A student may face such a choice in determining where to go to college. Rather than agonize about making the "best choice," it might be more conducive to peace of mind in the present and the future to simply say, "I don't know," and to choose what feels best or most natural. Or consider a person caught in the crossfire of a political debate. Rather than get all worked up about determining which side is correct, it might be more conducive to peace of mind to say, "I don't know," and suspend judgment. With the proliferation of news and information on TV and the internet, lots of people feel required to have a definite opinion about a vast number of subjects. But not everyone can truly care about or be well informed about every issue. The skeptic advises us to recognize this and to admit our own ignorance.

Often, we don't know in advance what will be for the good. When my father was forced into early retirement at age fifty-three, it seemed terrible. But if that had not happened he likely would have worked until sixty-five and still died, as he did, of cancer at sixty-nine. The way things worked out, he had several more years of enjoyable retirement. Often, we don't really know if a change or other occurrence is good until we consider it in the long run. The loss of a job or the breakup of a relationship may seem very bad in the short run, yet turn out to be the best thing that ever happened to us in the long run. The loss of a job can make me reconsider if that is really the line of work in which I want to spend my life and can thus inspire me to look for something better. The breakup of a relationship, which leaves me devastated at the moment, can turn out to be what I need to be free and to become my own person—the person who is then a good match for the person I will marry. Rather than react with strong emotions, I need to pause and say, "Maybe it's a good thing or maybe it's a bad thing. Only time will tell, and I will do my best to make a good thing out of it."

Finding the proper application of skepticism can be difficult, though. If the stories are to be believed, Pyrrho seems often to have taken things too far, nearly walking over cliffs and nearly getting run down by carts. But other stories are told of Pyrrho that suggest he was not always able to maintain his calm and uncertainty. He was embarrassed, for example, when friends found him fighting off a dog. Why not just treat the dog's existence as uncertain? The force of circumstances overrode the philosophical attitude. And that seems appropriate. We cannot and should not express and live out the implications of radical doubt on all subjects on all occasions. Applying the lessons of skepticism is a matter of personal judgment. As previously noted, some people do not deal well with the experience of doubt and uncertainty. I can identify with that. I would much prefer to have the feeling of security that came with my childhood faith. My mistake came in trying to replace the certainty of faith with the certainty of atheism. Later, honest reflection showed me that atheism cannot truly offer certainty, and so I found myself back in the question: for me, God is a question, not an answer. The poet Rainer Maria Rilke wisely counseled, "Be patient toward all that is unsolved in your heart and try to love the *questions themselves* like locked rooms and like books that are now written in a very foreign tongue. Do not now seek the answers, which cannot be given you because you would not be able to live them. And the point is, to live everything. *Live* the questions now. Perhaps you will then gradually, without noticing it, live along some distant day into the answer" (emphasis in the original).[14]

At times I find peace of mind in the skeptic's response to God: "I don't know," and so I suspend judgment. But more often I struggle with the question in the attempt to find an answer. This struggle can be uncomfortable and unnerving, but, for me, most of the time it is a source of pleasure. It's a kind of puzzle pleasure, like the kind one gets from reading a detective story or doing a crossword puzzle. But, in a way, that comparison trivializes the pleasure. For me it's more than a puzzle, it's a way of life. Concern for philosophical questions about God, the meaning of life, and the way to live most happily constitute the good life. Of course, I recognize that this kind of life doesn't appeal to, and wouldn't be enjoyed by, everyone, but it works for me. And I suspect that it would work for more people than just those who realize it.

There is a saying in the military that instructs us to "embrace the suck." The idea is that tasks or conditions may be far from ideal or far from desirable. Complaining about tasks and conditions that cannot be changed will do no good, though. One way to deal with such tasks or conditions is to throw oneself into them wholeheartedly, or in other words, to "embrace the suck." Clearly this applies to the human condition of doubt and uncertainty. It will do no good to complain about it or pretend that it isn't so. If, however, we embrace the uncertainty, we may find that it isn't as bad as we thought. Some of us may even enjoy the puzzle-solving it calls for.

Rather than compare living in the question to solving puzzles, though, we might better compare it to athletic training. Some people shake their heads in dismay at other people who run every morning. For the head-shakers, the last thing they feel like doing in the morning is going outside and physically exerting themselves. And so people who run appear to be masochists. In fact, there may be some truth to this observation. For at least some runners, there is pain involved, and the experience of the pain is part of the package. It is not, though, merely a matter of experiencing pain. Yes, there may be mental pain in overcoming inertia and resisting the temptation to stay in a warm bed. Yes, there may be physical pain, or at least displeasure, at some stage or stages of the run. But the run is also a matter of pleasure, often in a sense of being in the zone or experiencing flow in the activity, and in the sense of overcoming inertia and resistance to do what is hard. The sense of satisfaction derives not just from doing the activity once, but from doing it repeatedly, from having made it a habit, from turning something difficult into something second nature. Running, training, exercising become part of a healthy way of life. Likewise, living in the question, doubting, seeking, and wondering, can become part of a healthy way of life.

3

WHAT DO YOU MEAN BY "GOD"?

World history is full of gods, spanning continents and millennia. Most people do not believe in nearly any of those gods. In fact, this vast profusion of deities counts as evidence against any particular one of them being real. All cultures in all times and places have had their gods, and we readily recognize that people in those cultures were mistaken in their beliefs. So what reason do people have here and now to think they are different, that they are correct in the belief in their God?

There is another way of looking at the profusion of gods, however. Perhaps none of them is right in the details, but all of them are right in their basic insight. This kind of religious pluralism can be appealing. According to the philosophical theologian John Hick, "Pluralism is the view that the great world faiths embody different perceptions or conceptions of, and correspondingly different responses to, the Real or the Ultimate from within the major variant cultural ways of being human; and that within each of them the transformation of human existence from self-centeredness to Reality-centeredness is manifestly taking place—and taking place, so far as human observation can tell, to much the same extent."[1] In Kantian terms, Hick explains that "The Real is not experienced *an sich*, but in terms of various non-personal images or concepts that have been generated at the interface between the Real and different patterns of human consciousness."[2] In other words, no one experiences God, or the Real, exactly as he/she/ it is. Cultures and religions act as channels to God, but they also act as filters. Thus, for example, the monotheistic religions of the West approach God as masculine, whereas other religions, notably Hinduism, provide opportunity to approach the divine as feminine as well as masculine. Indeed, the human desire for devotion to the feminine divine is older than all major world religions and finds contemporary expression in Wicca, a pagan religious movement.

For the pluralist, our perception and understanding of God is always partial and imperfect. A version of a traditional Indian tale makes the same point simply and vividly. Several blind men feel an elephant and describe it. One man feels the trunk and says an elephant is long and narrow; another feels the tail and says an elephant is short and thin; another feels the ears and says an elephant is thin and flat; and so on. The point is that each of them is correct in their description of part of the elephant, but they are mistaken in thinking that they are describing the elephant as a whole. There really is an elephant, but they can't fully comprehend it. Perhaps we are like the blind men when we describe God. Perhaps there really is something there, but perhaps our ability to grasp it is severely limited.

This would be odd, of course. We can understand why the blind men can't come up with an accurate description of the elephant. But if God is the creator, why wouldn't he, she, or it have equipped us with the ability to know and understand God accurately? There may be no fully satisfactory answer to this question. It is sad to imagine that human beings have been groping for God for millennia like blind people examining an elephant. Of course the blind men could compare notes and put together a fuller account. And there would be nothing stopping a particular blind man from feeling all the different parts of the elephant and putting together his account of the whole.

So maybe that is what we are supposed to do: examine the teachings of all religions to search out commonalities to see where the beliefs of one supplement the beliefs of another. This can be a noble scholarly enterprise, but it is far too much to expect every person to do. Nor does it have great promise for arriving at truth. In the case of the Indian story, the blind men can be sure that they are feeling something. We, on the other hand, cannot be sure. We cannot know that there is a God whose true nature is captured imperfectly by various religions. It could all just be wishful thinking or projections of the fears and anxieties of the prescientific peoples who first articulated the world's religions.

Even if there were some prospect of success in assembling the parts of the truth glimpsed by the world's religions, this approach would not have much appeal to most followers of particular religions. After all, most religions are not open to the possibility that they see only part of the truth and that another religion may see another, perhaps more important, part of the truth. For example, Christianity and Islam claim exclusivity: you cannot be a Christian and a Muslim at the same time. Although some liberal Christians and Muslims will say that they ultimately worship the same God, they nonetheless believe incompatible things about that God. Notably, they disagree about the divinity of Jesus, and there is no way for that dispute to be settled to the satisfaction of all.

Other religions are not as insistent on exclusivity. Hinduism can readily accommodate other religions by recognizing their gods as part of the pantheon of gods. So a Hindu could admire Jesus and even recognize his divinity without ceasing to be a Hindu; it's just that most Christians would be unwilling to recognize this Hindu as a Christian because he holds on to polytheistic Hindu beliefs.

But the polytheism of Hinduism may be illusory on some interpretations. By some counts there are millions of gods recognized by different Hindus. Ultimately, though, one God is most important: Brahman. The insight most Hindus aim to achieve is that atman is Brahman. Atman is the soul, and the individual soul is one with God. Separation is an illusion; unity is the underlying truth. We are not truly separated from one another or from God, and the gods are not truly separate from one another. Various gods take on different forms or avatars. For example, the god Vishnu appears as his avatar Krishna in the *Bhagavad Gita*. Krishna is Vishnu. But on a deeper level Vishnu is Brahman. We are all Brahman. Reality is fundamentally one and unified. It is a lovely thought, but there is no good reason or argument to believe it is true or correct. Instead, there is tradition and religious authority.

Buddhism, which breaks away from Hinduism much as Christianity breaks away from Judaism, holds that nothing should be taken on faith or authority. All things should be tested. Many Buddhists accept the existence of gods, but not all do. While Buddhists have their own ways of stressing our interconnectedness, they reject the existence of atman, an individual soul. They would not say that atman is Brahman, because there is no atman (and there is no Brahman). Like Hinduism, Buddhism is very accommodating, readily taking on elements of, and associations with, other religions. As Buddhism spread from India, it took on elements of Taoism in China and became Zen in Japan. As it spread to Europe and America, Buddhism was assimilated by some Christians who found value in its meditative practice. Many Jews, including Jewish atheists, have also taken to Buddhism. Buddhism's lack of insistence on particular views of the divine and its willingness to change and adapt have made it attractive as a philosophy that can be readily combined with other religions. In response to the question—What do you mean by "God"?—Buddhism has no fixed answer.

Because the major monotheistic religions of the West—Judaism, Christianity, and Islam—have rigid views of God, they are more easily rejected, by one another and by nonbelievers. All of them claim a certain amount of mystery and unknowability concerning God, but they all nonetheless insist on enough specifics to generate skeptical response. All, for example, are subject to the problem of evil. Because they insist that God is all-loving and all-powerful, they have a difficult time explaining the existence of evil in the world. Yes, much evil results from human free will, and free will is itself ultimately a good thing. But there is also natural evil—the kind that does not result from human free will, such as earthquakes, plagues, and disease. The child who suffers from leukemia has done nothing to deserve it, and surely an all-powerful God could have made a world without leukemia (or earthquakes or AIDS or the common cold, for that matter).

Some philosophers and theologians invest prodigious amounts of time, energy, and intelligence in attempting to reconcile the existence of natural evil with the existence of an all-loving, all-powerful God. Most of these arguments boil down to the claim that our limited human perspective does not allow us to view the big picture in which these supposedly evil things are actually good. With such arguments, philosophers and theologians may occasionally impress one another, but they have yet to come up with an argument that would move the nonbeliever to reconsider. The American philosopher William James, himself a Christian, says, "So much for the metaphysical attributes of God! From the point of view of practical religion, the metaphysical monster which they offer to our worship is an absolutely worthless invention of the scholarly mind."[3]

Perhaps, like James, believers should reconsider their conception of God. The problem of evil arises only for an all-loving, all-powerful God. By contrast, the gods of most times and places have only been very powerful and somewhat loving. Take the Greek gods, for example. They are simply overgrown, super-powered human beings, with all of our faults and most of our problems. They are petty, jealous, and envious, taking sides in human wars and meddling in human affairs. Zeus constantly cheats on his wife and often gets caught. The Greeks had no philosophical or theological worry about why famine, disease, and natural disasters struck. The gods were not all-powerful, nor did the gods love humanity to an extent that would motivate them to always prevent such things. The details differ, but the bottom line remains for other gods in most times and places: they are not all-powerful and all-loving.

But surely things are different in the great monotheistic religions of the West. Not so. The God of Abraham in the Old Testament is depicted as angry, jealous, and vengeful. Far from being all-powerful or all-loving, he can't even seem to control his own temper. To the extent that Judaism, Christianity, and Islam accept this Old Testament depiction as accurate, they find themselves with a God who is not all-loving and all-powerful. It is the God of the philosophers rather than the God of scripture that is supposed to be all-loving and all-powerful. There seem to have been no claims among ancient Israelites that their God was all-loving and all-powerful, and it's not clear that early Christians would have made those claims either. From a Jewish perspective, Yoram Hazony says,

> It's hard to find any evidence that the prophets and scholars who wrote the Hebrew Bible (or "Old Testament") thought of God in this way [perfect, all-good and all-powerful] at all. The God of Hebrew Scripture is not depicted as immutable, but repeatedly changes his mind about things (for example, he regrets having made man).

He is not all-knowing, since he's repeatedly surprised by things (like the Israelites abandoning him for a statue of a cow). He is not perfectly powerful either, in that he famously cannot control Israel and get its people to do what he wants. And so on.[4]

At the risk of oversimplifying a complex historical development, the all-loving, all-powerful God seems to have resulted from Christian interpretation and application of Plato. The Greek philosopher believed the world that we know through the senses is but a pale shadow of a higher reality of perfect Forms, the most important of which is the Form of the Good. Augustine, the first great Christian philosopher, was deeply influenced by Plato via his later followers, the Neoplatonists. For Augustine, Plato's perfect Forms became ideas in the mind of God, and God himself was perfect goodness as well as perfect love. This line of thought was affirmed by later Christian philosophers and theologians like Anselm and Aquinas, for whom God was not just the greatest being there is, but the greatest being possible. He was thus all-loving and all-powerful.

There is something comforting about such a God, like the ultimate father figure, but there is also something unrelatable about such a God. How can he be approached or understood? What need has he for us? Humans have always created gods in their own image. In this case, male philosophers and theologians created a God in the image of what they aspired to be. Most other people never really bought the image, though, as evidenced by the practice of petitionary prayer, which commonly takes the form of a bargain: I'll worship you if you do things for me. This was the essence of the exclusive contract Abraham signed with God. The God of the Old Testament really wanted a people to call his own and who would worship him exclusively. Throughout the ages, humans have petitioned God with prayer, asking for good weather, healthy children, favorable business outcomes, and so on. In return they have offered their worship and their promise to act the way God wanted them to act. The implicit message is that it's a pain to worship God and follow his rules, but it's worth the trade-off if (and only if) God comes through with some rewards. A God that would engage in this kind of horse trading may be loving and powerful, but he is not all-loving and all-powerful.

Perhaps it is time to rethink the conception of God, to abandon what the philosopher John D. Caputo calls the "old palace God"[5] and return to a God who more closely resembles humanity. Perhaps God is a bumbler or a slacker, not as bad as us, but not unlike us. That would explain a lot. It would explain disease, famine, and earthquakes. God wasn't capable of making a world any better than the one we have, and he isn't able to do anything to improve it. The philosopher David Hume, for example, considered the possibility that this world was the imperfect attempt of a young and inexperienced God.[6] But that casts the matter in a negative light. Rather than focus on God's lack of power, it might be more helpful to focus on God's similarity to humanity. A God who makes mistakes and is unable to correct imperfections in his creation would be a God that humanity could more readily identify with, approach, and connect with. Or, as an alternative to an aloof father, we might conceive the divine as a welcoming mother. But, alas, that is not how God has revealed himself according to the monotheistic religions of the West.

In the Judeo-Christian tradition, God revealed himself to prophets long ago, but today his presence is revealed only indirectly, if at all. As Thomas Aquinas put it, God is *deus absconditus*, the hidden God—the God who absconds. The question is why. Why does God no longer reveal himself in grand fashion as he once did? The most common answer is that God wants us to believe on faith. He wants us to come to know him through our own efforts, rather than as a result of being overwhelmed by his undeniable presence. This is a much harder road to travel, and many people reject it. Would it really be so bad to be shown clear and undeniable signs of God's existence? Would it really overwhelm us to the extent that we would be deprived of our freedom to choose? It's hard to answer in the affirmative. The traditional stories of Adam and Eve, and even Lucifer's fall, illustrate the tendency to reject the divine even when in its very presence. Whatever God's reason is for hiding, we don't know it for sure—we are left guessing. It is akin to, or even part of, the problem of evil. We are left wondering why an all-loving God would do it. The ultimate answer seems to be that it is part of a bigger plan that we don't and can't fully understand.

There is another way to interpret God's absence: perhaps God is not an all-loving, all-powerful creator. Perhaps he's not even a struggling slacker. Perhaps God is simply a creative force that began the universe and left it alone. This image of the divine finds expression in the works of the ancient Greek philosopher Epicurus, who said that the gods were immortal and blessed but that they had no concern for humanity. In the philosophy of Epicurus, peace of mind is the highest goal, and, he reasoned, the gods would have the most perfect peace of mind. Thus he rejected the traditional depiction of the gods in Greek religion of his time. Gods did not take sides in human affairs, and, according to Epicurus, there was no reason to fear the gods. They do not punish us, nor do they reward us. Epicurus saw Greek religion as harmful because it inspired fear of the gods' wrath in this life or the next. Beyond that, Epicurus conceived of the human being as purely physical, and he rejected any thought of an afterlife. Rather, he argued that this life is all we have and thus we should live it in pursuit of the highest pleasure, peace of mind.

This Epicurean conception of the divine was resurrected in the Enlightenment philosophy of deism. Inspired by the great success of the scientific revolution and the increasingly mechanistic appearance of the cosmos, one type of deism depicts a clockmaker God who made the universe so that it runs on its own and then left it alone. This is not the *deus absconditus* of Aquinas; this is *deus otiosus*—the God who has withdrawn from creation, who is outside and apart from creation. He or she or it may have been benevolent in the initial act of creation, but now is no longer involved or perhaps even aware. In this sense, God comes to be just a name or placeholder for the first cause, the initial starting point. In the contemporary sense, we may point to the big bang and ask what came before that. Wherever the stopping point is for our series of questions and answers, that stopping point is God, at least according to one type of deism.

At this point, God bears so little resemblance to the God of the major monotheistic religions that one has to wonder what is so objectionable. What is to be gained by insisting that there is no God even in this sense, even in this watered-down version so divorced from religion? Of course, it may turn out that there is no God even in this sense, but such a God would not involve any contradictions or any apparent conflicts with evidence or experience. Such a God wouldn't do much, but he or she or it would at least answer the question, Why is there a universe? Why is there something rather than nothing? The answer would be that a divine creator made it. This would not be to insist that he or she or it made it out of love or for any particular reason. Of course, if such a God had no particular reason for making the universe, that amounts to saying that there is no reason for the universe in the sense of no predetermined purpose for the universe.

Such a conception of God will leave many people cold. Seizing on the idea that we don't know anything for certain about God, and observing that different cultures across times and places have had very different conceptions of God, some people will decide to choose their own conception of God. After all, the various options at Starbucks allow for over 87,000 different ways to get your coffee. Why shouldn't there be as many or more ways to get your God? Why not choose the combination that suits your taste?

4

RELIGIOUS FICTIONALISM

It is tempting to interpret the tale of the blind men and the elephant from chapter 3 as an endorsement of relativism: the view that all accounts of God are equally true or valid, and so we should feel free to choose or create our own conception of God. This is not the intended message of the story, however. Rather, the message is one of humility: we are always limited in our experience and description of the divine, and so we should not think we have a monopoly on truth and we should not automatically reject the accounts of others as foolish. This is not only a message of humility, but one of tolerance and freedom.

Safe in the knowledge that no one has the whole truth, we are free to form our own picture of the divine. To some extent people have always done this. For example, part of the grandeur of Hinduism is its vast proliferation of gods and rituals. There is room within the religion for the expression of personal devotion to particular deities and particular avatars. Indeed, what we call Hinduism may not be a single religion, but many. Likewise, animistic and pagan religions are usually expansive enough to allow for individual tailoring, with focus on a particular god or cult. The polytheism of ancient Greece comes to mind. A priest of Apollo, or devotee of Athena, or cultic follower of Dionysus did not reject the rest of the religion and pantheon, but he did focus his worship in a particular way that was different from the run of the mill. Very likely, most pagans had some particular focus in their religious devotion, perhaps focused on a local deity, or a family deity, or a deity associated with a particular profession.

This is part of what made it difficult for Christianity to supplant paganism: the idea that one God could do the work of the many was not intuitively obvious to pagans. Christianity thus preserved the plurality of paganism; minor deities on whom people counted could be replaced by saints. Saints weren't exactly gods, but they did have the ear of God. They could and would intercede on your behalf. Thus Christianity, which sought to tame its own incipient pluralism with a single creed, never fully succeeded. Most people have always preferred to have some degree of choice; they prefer a spiritual cafeteria to a fixed menu. Still, some people have preferred the fixed menu. Indeed, an unswerving, unalterable orthodoxy has always been attractive to some people. The certainty that comes with rigidity is, no doubt, a source of comfort and righteousness.

Perhaps more often for political reasons—for centralizing power and authority—than for spiritual reasons, religions have sought to codify orthodox belief and practice. But the history of splits and schisms within religions shows that this has not been entirely successful. Then again, the strict orthodoxy that is abandoned is often replaced by a new, no less strict orthodoxy. Still, historically intrepid groups and individuals mustered the courage to break away from the orthodox group and make a space to practice their religion as they saw fit. Far more common must have been people who remained within the orthodoxy but privately carved out a space for their personal spiritual practice, expression, and devotion. Despite the effort to replace minor deities with saints, Christianity never fully conquered paganism. Folk practices, witchcraft, and spells remained. While not all Christians indulged or believed in such pagan practices, for many Christians some elements of non-Christian superstition lingered.

For most of human history, we have been limited in the cafeteria selection from which we could choose. In most times and places, most people would never have met a practitioner of another religion. And ideas could spread only very slowly. With the printing press, that began to change. People had the chance to read about other religions very different from their own. All of this accelerated and spread over time as more and more people became literate and books became more widely available. The internet, of course, has brought this to new heights. Anyone with an internet connection can learn about other religions with a click or a tap.

One reaction to the profusion of religious information is to conclude that it is all nonsense. Surely, some of it is nonsense; maybe most or nearly all of it is nonsense. So, why think that any of it is worthwhile? Why not relegate it all to the trash can? The vast majority of gods and religions have not survived even to be documented on Wikipedia. They have gone to the trash can, and the trash can has been emptied, its contents never to be found again. This seems to be the way of all things, the march of historical inevitability. The religions that now remain will be documented for posterity, but why think that they will survive outside Wikipedia? Perhaps they won't. But not everyone has this reaction to the profusion.

Some people see the expanded cafeteria selection as an opportunity to assemble the spiritual meal that suits them best. Far from scorning all the dishes on offer, they see a bountiful blessing. Each of us is now free to make our own God, the way we might make our own sundae by choosing from among thirty-eight flavors of ice cream and a dizzying array of toppings. We can't eat them all, but we can find what we like best, and that too can change from one time to the next. Because there's no disputing taste, why should I turn my nose up at the combination you have concocted for your sundae God? If you like it, good for you. Tolerance is the overriding virtue. As long as you are tolerant and don't inflict harm on others, then you have earned similar treatment in return. Live and let live.

All of this would be fine, if we were really just talking about sundaes. Sundaes are real, after all. But the metaphysical options on offer at the religious buffet may not be real. Many of them almost certainly are not. Still, what harm could come from such indulgence? No tooth decay or weight gain will result. And if it is all done in a spirit of tolerance, it seems harmless and perhaps beneficial. After all, we routinely sample from the fictional options on offer at the movies, on television, and in bookstores. If the selections at the religious cafeteria turned out to be just as fictional as Star Wars, what would be the problem? Part of the problem would be that there would be no way to arbitrate disputes and disagreements, or at least no valid way. If all religious beliefs were equally false, all equally based in fiction, there would be no legitimate way to settle disputes among them, no legitimate way of saying which would be best. Of course, we could point to consequences. Some religious beliefs might do a better job of alleviating suffering in the world; some might do a better job of producing inner peace.

This is part of the allure of choosing from the postmodern buffet. "To each his own" is the dominant attitude. No one is in a position to dispute or disprove another. There is even the prevailing belief that "it's all relative." Because so many beliefs about God cannot be ultimately proven or disproven, they are taken to be all true, or to be true relative to the individual. What is true for me is not true for you, and that is fine. The problem is that it's not fine. Truth is not relative in this way. Only belief is relative in this way. I believe one thing and you believe another, but that does not make both of our beliefs true. Beliefs can contradict one another. If person A believes that Jesus is God and person B believes there is no God but Allah, then their beliefs contradict one another. The beliefs cannot both be true, though they could both be false. Relativism ignores metaphysical facts because those metaphysical facts are hard or impossible to access or know. But either there is a God or there is not a God. There is a metaphysical fact at issue; it is just that it is difficult or impossible to know in any absolute sense. Either there is a prime number greater than ninety and less than ninety-three or there is not. There is a metaphysical fact of the matter, and there is a right and a wrong answer to the question. It's just that it's much easier to determine the answer to the mathematical question than the God question.

What if the answer turns out to be that there is no God? Then all the people building their own God at the religious sundae bar are deluding themselves. They are living in a fantasy world without knowing it or realizing it. To the extent that their religious beliefs help them to live, perhaps this is a good thing. When Karl Marx called religion the opium of the people, he did not mean to disparage the people or religion. He meant to comment on the state of the world. In a less frequently quoted line he also called religion "the heart of a heartless world."[1] Of course it would be better to do without the opium, but given the state of the world, who could blame anyone for indulging in it? It might even be a good or necessary thing, like the anesthesia needed for surgery. But this is not to say that we should rest content with the opium of religion, at least not all of us. Instead, we should be motivated to change the world so as to make the opium unnecessary. This is what Marx sought to do, and even if we do not agree with the particulars of his plan, we can salute his motivation. The opium analogy breaks down to the extent that the person taking opium knows he is creating a false reality. Of course, not all drug users realize they are creating a false reality. Some may argue just the opposite—that the drug allows them to see reality more purely and truly. Some may deny their dependence on the drug. By contrast, the religious believer is less likely to realize the extent to which his belief creates a false view of reality. He is more likely to be like the drug user who denies an insidious dependence and claims that the drug allows him to see reality more truly and purely.

But what about the person who has come to disbelieve in the existence of God and the truth of religion and who continues to indulge in the opium? What about the *fictionalist*? Following a fictionalist account of God, we would *accept* statements like "God exists" while *not believing* they are true. As a result, we would act as if it were true that "God exists," but when pushed to give our genuine answer to the question of whether there is a God, we would say no. Fictionalism is disingenuous, encouraging us to turn a blind eye to what we really believe. It may not be the most pernicious kind of self-deception, but it is self-deception nonetheless. We find a person's engagement with movies and novels commendable only if the person does not spend more time in those fictional worlds than outside them. But in the case of religious fictionalism the person is spending nearly all of his time in a fictionalized world—only coming out of it briefly when he considers the philosophical question of the existence of God.

Perhaps the religious fictionalist can be justified, though. Perhaps it is literally false that God exists and yet it is mythologically true, conveying a deep truth despite being literally false. Religious fictionalists accept the existence of God, but they do not really believe God exists. They accept that God is love and that (the concept of) God has shaped human history and guides human lives, but when pinned down they admit that they do not really believe in the actual existence of such a God. Their considered judgment is that the existence of God is not literally true but rather is mythologically true.[2]

As an example, the philosopher Jean Kazez says, "I am a religious fictionalist. I don't just banish all religious sentences to the flames. I make believe some of them are true, and I think that's all to the good. . . . at our Seder . . . I pretended there was a deity to be praised for various things. I also pretended the Jews were once slaves in Egypt, and were liberated with the help of a powerful deity who ushered them into the land of Israel (after making them wander in the desert for 40 years)."[3] It seems as though Kazez's fictionalism is voluntary; she cultivates it. Perhaps it is an attempt to game the system, to gain some of the benefits of religious belief without actually believing. There may be cultural benefits, as in the benefits of celebrating the Seder that Kazez describes. There may also be moral benefits. Some people may find it easier to behave morally if they pretend that there is a God who is watching them. Pretending to believe can work, not necessarily because God will magically intercede on our behalf, but because pretending to believe in God will make things go our way by predisposing us to do the things we need to do to make things go our way. In a similar way we could pretend that taking a vitamin C pill every morning will prevent colds even though we do not really believe it. Taking the pill could act as a reminder that we are committed to washing hands regularly, eating properly, and doing all we can to prevent colds.

Kazez's religious fictionalism sounds voluntary, but perhaps for some people religious fictionalism is involuntary. For whatever reason, they cannot help but act as if there were a God, even though, when they stop to consider the matter, they do not really believe God exists. When a novel or movie is particularly engrossing, our reactions to it may be involuntary and resistant to our attempts to counter them. We form what the philosopher Tamar Szabó Gendler calls *aliefs*, automatic belief-like attitudes that contrast with our well-considered beliefs.[4] For example, despite our beliefs that it is only a movie and that the characters are not real, because of our aliefs, we end up screaming when the monster jumps out at the heroine from behind a tree.

What if some cases of religious fictionalism are like our involuntary screams in the theater? What if there are cases of *involuntary religious fictionalism*? Cultural indoctrination might play a role. To some extent it may be difficult to erase the programming from earlier in life. For example, although I am no longer a believing Catholic, I still sometimes feel a twinge of guilt when I eat meat on a Friday during Lent. More broadly, it makes sense that someone who is raised in a family and a culture that emphasizes belief in God will have a lingering sense of belief.

In his moving memoir, *Hoping Against Hope: Confessions of a Postmodern Pilgrim*, John D. Caputo describes his Catholic education and upbringing, his time in a monastery, his career as a Catholic philosopher engaged with postmodern thought, and his current view that God does not exist—rather, God "insists." Caputo came to reject the "economics" of salvation[5] and even the existence of God. Yet God remained and remains for Caputo. As he says, "The insistence of God means there is something to God, but that does not mean God exists. It means God insists, that something is going on in the name of God. It is not that there is a Supreme Being up there to reckon with—but that there is something going on."[6] Caputo's view is more robust than Kazez's voluntary fictionalism. Caputo is not pretending; he is feeling the real force of the concept of God while nonetheless recognizing that there is no actual God. By "insist" Caputo means "something that does not quite exist but still makes itself felt; something that calls upon us, lures us, solicits us."[7] So the concept or idea of God is real and impactful even if God does not exist. As Caputo says,

> God's inexistence is the condition under which the conditions of the world are transformed, shocked, and jolted by an excessive demand that seems positively unreal, like a pure gift, or pure hospitality, or pure forgiveness. The insistence of God means that the name of God is something that lays claim to us unconditionally, like a promise of things that eye has not seen nor ears heard, but without the force of being, power, sovereignty, and omnipotence. It means that something calls upon us unconditionally, but without the power of an economic system of rewards or retributions or an army, even without a heavenly host of angels, to back it up.[8]

Perhaps Caputo has arrived at the destination of his religious and intellectual journey, or perhaps he will move further along the continuum and simply embrace atheism. He tells us, after all, that "God is an atheist" and "God dares not to be."[9] Perhaps, though, Caputo has simply gone as far in the direction of atheism as he could, considering his early environment and upbringing.

It is not just cultural indoctrination that can lead to involuntary religious fictionalism, however. We may be biologically hardwired to believe in God even when we have dismissed God as a fiction. Human beings evolved to have an overactive theory of mind, seeing purpose, intention, and teleology where there is none. The phrase "theory of mind" simply refers to the ability to think about what other people are thinking. Children normally develop this ability by around age four, and it is crucial for success in human society. Humans survive not by strength or speed—other animals greatly surpass us in these—but by cooperation. Successful cooperation involves not just linguistic communication, but the ability to think about what other people are thinking, a theory of mind. Can this other person be trusted to cooperate and help, or will he turn and defect?

The process of natural selection is often scattershot rather than precise. In this case it has not simply endowed us with the tendency to think about what other people are thinking, but about what other animals and things are thinking. Evolution can lead to false beliefs when those false beliefs favor the survival of our genes. As a fisherman, I know about this overactive theory of mind. I imagine the fish thinking about me in the boat, trying to outwit me by stealing my bait. In reality, the thought process of the fish is nowhere near that sophisticated. More comically and pathetically, I find myself getting angry at my computer when it doesn't run properly, as if it were out to get me, as if it were a fickle friend or lover who had to be coaxed into behaving the way I want. I react this way to the computer involuntarily, even though upon reflection I know that the computer has no mind, has no motivations. Hardwired human nature has us looking for motivations everywhere, and we are stuck with this hardwiring, even though we could benefit from an upgrade that would allow us to look for motivations more selectively, filtering out bad candidates. In *The Belief Instinct*, the atheist psychologist Jesse Bering explains that

> Just as we see other people as more than just their bodies, we also tend to see natural events as more than natural events. And again, this seeing beyond the obvious is the consequence of the very peculiar way our brains have evolved, with a theory of mind. At every turn, we seem to think there are subtle messages scratched into the woodwork of nature, subtle signs or cues that God, or some other supernatural agent, is trying to communicate a lesson or idea to us—and often to us alone. Usually, it's about how we should behave. So we listen attentively, effortlessly translating natural events into divine or supernatural messages.[10]

Bering hypothesizes that our overactive theory of mind both created God and sustains him. We saw purpose and intention everywhere. The rain could mean that the gods were happy or it could mean that the gods were angry. What it could not mean was nothing at all—we were not naturally equipped to look at the world that way. Science, though, has helped us. Modern science has banished teleology; it does not look for purposes. Rather it looks for mechanical causes and effects. Yet even the most rigorous scientist may find herself getting mad at her computer.

Likewise, even a committed atheist, who is convinced on rational grounds that God does not exist, may nonetheless find herself involuntarily wondering about God's thoughts or intentions. As Bering says, "There's reason to believe that, even for the committed atheist, the voice of God is still annoyingly there, though perhaps reduced to no more than a whisper."[11] The existentialist philosopher Jean-Paul Sartre famously described the human as the being for whom existence precedes essence. A human-made product like a can opener has an essence even before it exists. That is, the manufacturer has a design and purpose in mind even before she makes the can opener. But because there is no God, Sartre reasoned, the human being has no essence prior to existence. Yes, we have DNA that makes us biologically human, but unlike other living things we do not simply obey the dictates of DNA and instincts. Rather, through our own choices we give ourselves a purpose, an essence. We don't have a pre-given plan or purpose; there is no individually given meaning of life. As Bering describes it, to say "that you or I exist for a reason, would constitute an obvious category error, one in which we're applying teleo-functional thinking to something that neither was designed creatively nor evolved as a discrete biological adaptation."[12]

We are what we make of ourselves. No one was more committed to this line of thought than Sartre. There is no plan or purpose for us; we are not fulfilling our destiny. And yet, in conversation with Simone de Beauvoir, Sartre said, "I don't see myself as so much dust that has appeared in the world, but as a being that was expected, prefigured, called forth. In short, as a being that could, it seems, come only from a creator . . . It contradicts many of my other ideas. But it is there, floating vaguely. And when I think of myself I often think rather in this way, for want of being able to think otherwise."[13] In his autobiography, *The Words* (*Les Mots*), Sartre at first claims to have become a resolute atheist at age twelve, but then later in the book he says, "Atheism is a cruel and long-range affair: I think I've carried it through."[14] As John Gillespie explains, "Sartre's relation to the Death of God is therefore ambiguous. Because of the difficulties it poses, the temptation must always be resisted, so God is constantly present in his thoughts in His absence, and is not yet dead."[15]

Ironically, at moments of extreme cognitive dissonance, Sartre may have seen his God-given purpose as involving the spread of atheism. Of course, he would have dismissed such thoughts in the next moment, but as a good philosopher he must have allowed himself some doubt. Perhaps he was wrong about God. This lingering thought of God, this momentary involuntary fictionalism, does not do anything to prove the existence of God. In fact, it is easily accounted for in terms of a biological explanation, an imprecisely evolved, overactive theory of mind. Right?

5

IS FAITH A GIFT?

Faith is often dismissed as simply believing against evidence. The neuroscientist and atheist Sam Harris, for example, writes that "Religious faith is the belief in historical and metaphysical propositions without sufficient evidence. When the evidence for a religious proposition is thin or nonexistent, or there is compelling evidence against it, people invoke faith."[1] If this is what faith is, then Harris and others are right to dismiss it and even condemn it.

Let's consider, though, whether this may be an unfair or incomplete depiction. Perhaps for the person of genuine faith, faith itself is another way of knowing. Perhaps faith provides sufficient basis for belief, and perhaps that basis is not restricted to evidence as a scientist would conceive of it. Because there are highly intelligent and highly educated people, including some leading scientists, who believe that faith is a way of knowing that gives them access to the divine, we need to keep open to the possibility. Hamlet's admonition comes to mind: "There are more things in heaven and earth, Horatio, / Than are dreamt of in your philosophy."

Knowledge requires justification, and from a scientific standpoint justification involves evidence. But perhaps we can have justification without evidence. Perhaps there is another way of knowing certain things that does not involve observation, reason, and testing. The mathematician and mystic Blaise Pascal famously said that "the heart has its reasons of which reason knows nothing."[2] This is the core of the issue: Is there a way of knowing that operates apart from reason? Concerning God, is faith a way of sensing the divine, a *sensus divinitatis*? More questions follow: Is it a gift? Is the gift lacking in some people completely? Is it weak or obscured in some people? Is it just particularly strong in some people?

Speaking of a faithful Jew named Sol, an unnamed woman at dinner in Woody Allen's *Crimes and Misdemeanors* says, "Sol's kind of faith is a gift. It's like an ear for music, or a talent to draw. He believes, and you can use logic on him all day and he still believes." The conception of faith as a gift or a talent is intriguing. We all recognize that some people have talents that others lack. As highlighted in the movie dialogue, such talents or gifts don't have to be productive like the ability to draw. Instead, they can be detective, like an ear for music. Not everyone has a particular gift, like the ability to draw or appreciate music, or at least not everyone has it without effort and development. Some of my friends seem to have ecstatic experiences beholding the beauty of nature. I like trees, and grass, and rocks, and mountains, and rivers, but they never take my breath away. Some people are able to detect subtleties of flavor in food that most of us miss. Such "supertasters" can earn a lot of money by offering their reactions to food companies that are determining which products to bring to market. Like most abilities, though, tasting can be developed. There are, for example, wine tasting classes. Not everyone can become an expert wine taster whose opinions are worth money, but nearly anyone can develop the ability to discern certain subtleties and make certain distinctions in tasting wine.

Perhaps faith is something like that, an ability that comes easily and naturally to some people and comes only with great difficulty for other people. On a related note, there are parts of the color spectrum that humans cannot see with the naked eye, and there are parts of the sound spectrum that humans cannot detect with the unaided ear. These parts of the color and sound spectrums are no less real for our inability to detect them directly. Perhaps faith puts a person in touch with part of the "spectrum of reality" that cannot be detected by unaided reason or observation.

The philosopher David Hume relays a story told by Sancho Panza in *Don Quixote*. A man and his brother claim to share a family ability to taste wine with great delicacy and discernment. The two brothers are asked to taste the wine from a particular hogshead and render their judgments. One brother tastes the wine and says it is good but it has a vague taste of leather; the other brother tastes the wine and says it is good but it has a vague taste of iron. The people laugh at the brothers who have rendered such different judgments. When the wine has been drunk to the bottom, though, they discover an iron key on a leather loop. Obviously both brothers were partially right; each was tasting something that the other missed and that everyone else missed altogether.[3] Perhaps faith is like that. Perhaps people with the gift or talent or ability of faith are able to detect something in the spectrum of reality that we would otherwise miss with an ordinary view. Perhaps no individual or group grasps the whole of reality, the whole truth. Along these lines, the scholar of world religions Wilfred Cantwell Smith says, "Truth is ultimately one, although the human forms of truth and the forms of faith decorate or bespatter our world diversely."[4] This is not to say that humans get a pass for falling short of grasping ultimate truth. We must still try: "One's conceptualizing of faith, and of the universe perceived from faith, if it is itself to be faithful, must be the closest approximation to the truth to which one is capable of rising (being raised)."[5]

When it comes to faith, perhaps we employ the wrong standards when we analyze propositions to confirm or deny their truth. People across continents and centuries have believed many different, even contradictory, things based on faith. But perhaps we miss something when we focus on the specifics of belief. Perhaps faith is believing *in*, not believing *that*. Stephen Batchelor says, "Faith is not equivalent to mere belief. Faith is the condition of ultimate confidence that we have the capacity to follow the path of doubt to its end."[6] The faiths of individuals or of particular religions are usually bound up with specific beliefs, but perhaps the specific beliefs are less important than the sense that one is in touch with a higher reality and that one is committed to that reality. To be sure, many individuals will insist that specific religious beliefs are of ultimate importance, but perhaps that insistence demonstrates a lack of faith. Indeed, Smith says, "A belief is far too historical and transient a phenomenon, too vulnerable, too *mundane*, to be confused with the object of faith."[7]

The content of belief, the *what* of belief, changes over centuries and across continents. Recognizing this, the Danish philosopher Søren Kierkegaard distinguished between the *what* of belief and the *how* of belief. For him, passion was of prime importance. Kierkegaard found the institutionalized Christianity of nineteenth-century Copenhagen to be dead and deadening. People showed up for church on Sunday and professed the proper beliefs, but then they went on with their lives without giving Christ another thought. Thus, for Kierkegaard, in a place where everyone is Christian, no one is Christian. The Christians of his native city had the *what* of belief, but they lacked the *how* of belief. They believed the doctrines of their religion with all the fervor that schoolchildren have for learning facts of arithmetic. This can be easily contrasted with the *how* of belief experienced by the early Christians. For these early Christians, there was great risk in the public profession of their faith, and there was great zeal in the urgency of spreading the good news, because they believed Christ would return soon. They were wrong about the imminence of the second coming, wrong in the *what* but not in the *how* of belief.

To recapture the passion and faith of early Christianity, Kierkegaard recommends reflecting on the absurdity of what Christians believe. He even echoes the early church father Tertullian, who is paraphrased as saying, "I believe because it is absurd."[8] On the face of it, this statement appears ridiculous: absurdity is a reason for *not* believing. But what Kierkegaard and Tertullian are saying is that belief worthy of the name, Belief with a capital *B*, the *how* of belief in terms of subjective passion, requires risk and objective uncertainty. Indeed, a belief that is absurd from an objective standpoint is the perfect catalyst to this kind of belief. Along similar lines, Miguel de Unamuno writes, "Those who believe that they believe in God, but without any passion in their heart, without anguish of mind, without uncertainty, without doubt, without an element of despair even in their consolation, believe only in the God-Idea, not in God himself."[9]

Kierkegaard was fond of musing on the apparent contradiction involved in a timeless God, a God outside the space and time he created, somehow entering space and time in the person of Jesus. But, of course, absurd Christian belief need not be so abstract. That Jesus was born of a virgin, that he performed miracles, and that he rose from the dead are all absurd beliefs from an objective standpoint. But when everyone in Copenhagen believes these things, no one really believes them. Everyone has the *what* of belief, but no one has the *how*. Everyone has belief, but no one has faith. Thus Kierkegaard contrasts two people: one goes to a Christian church and prays without passion, and the other lives in a pagan land and prays to an idol with all the passion of the infinite. The Christian in effect worships an idol, and the pagan in effect worships the true God.[10] To be in the truth is a matter of subjectivity, for Kierkegaard. The scientific realm is the place for detached objectivity, but the religious realm is the place for subjectivity—the place where feeling matters more than fact.

By decoupling faith from belief, Kierkegaard and others may want to exempt it from the evaluation as true or false in the usual sense. Faith is not to be judged in terms of the objective truth of the propositions it endorses. Faith is not true or false in the objective sense. Rather, faith is either genuine or not, perhaps misplaced or not. Smith says, "Faith is not belief in a doctrine. It is not even belief in the truth as such, whatever it be. It is 'assent' to the truth as such, in the dynamic and personal sense of rallying to it with delight and engagement. . . . It is the ability to see and to respond."[11] On this account, faith involves insight and response. Insight may, in part, be a gift or a talent. It requires more than simple knowing. By way of comparison, Smith suggests, "there is a difference between knowing that a joke is funny . . . and personally 'seeing the joke.'"[12] Or, one may believe that Bach's music is beautiful even if one is deaf or doesn't feel moved by the music oneself. In such a case, one has knowledge without insight.[13]

People without such faith are right, however, to cast a skeptical glance at it. Doubt is important, but it is also important to remain open. The sincerity of some faithful people should be enough to give the skeptic pause, and the importance of a kind of faith in other parts of life may give the skeptic reason to explore further. For example, consider the mother who has faith that her son is innocent despite the prosecutor's overwhelming evidence against him. Or, more trivially, consider the Cubs fan who had faith season after season that his team would win the World Series until it finally did in 2016.

The mundane examples of the mother and the Cubs fan illustrate that faith is more than just a matter of insight; it is also a matter of response. The mother does not just believe that her son is innocent; she responds and takes action. She is committed and faithful, putting up bail for her son and mortgaging her house to pay lawyers for her son's defense.

The Cubs fan doesn't just believe his team will win. He is a faithful fan, committed to his team. He goes to Wrigley Field and roots for the home team; he wears a Cubs hat to show his support. Even when he is alone watching the game on television, he responds to the events on the field as if his actions as a fan could make a difference. It has been said that faith without works is dead (James 2:14–26). Perhaps, though, we could say it is not faith at all if there are no works, no actions taken in response. This is not to say that all responses will be effective. The Cubs fan will have no effect on the outcome of the game on the field by performing superstitious rituals home alone. At best, such rituals bolster affection for the team and encourage other actions that could help the team, however indirectly and infinitesimally.

The Cubs fan may seem to lack insight, but consider what Smith says, that "religious faith intellectually is first of all the ability to see the point of a tradition."[14] Here is the insight: the Cubs fan sees that there is something valuable and worthwhile in rooting for the Cubs and performing all the rituals involved. Not everyone living in the city of Chicago has this insight, and certainly not everyone in Chicago responds to it with the devotion of a true, faithful Cubs fan. Insight distinguishes faith from mere loyalty or blind devotion, which may result from a simple sense of obligation.

There are, of course, other teams, much as there are other religions. The Cubs fan is not a Red Sox fan, but he can appreciate the faith of the Red Sox fan and maybe even learn from it and gather hope from it—the Red Sox too won a World Series after a long drought. Despite what separates them, the Cubs fan and the Red Sox fan share much in common and may even be taking different paths to essentially the same experience. As Smith says of religious faith, "truth transcends our insight into it."[15] Perhaps we only glimpse truth partially and imperfectly through the lens of our particular tradition or religion. But despite our limited view, we can take valuable action in response. For this reason, Smith says, "Faith is a virtue. Believing is not."[16] Back to baseball, we can understand this by saying that it is what the Cubs fan and the Red Sox fan share in common, their faith, that is a virtue, not their specific beliefs about their teams. To paraphrase Kierkegaard, when everyone is a Cubs fan, no one is a Cubs fan. It is not the profession of beliefs or the surface-level actions that matter. It is a deeper devotion that makes the difference. Perhaps I've extended this baseball analogy too far. But whether or not being a Cubs fan involves having faith, it clearly does involve some kind of insight and response. Not everyone living in Chicago will have the same insight and the same devotion, but an openness to the Cubs will inspire the insight and commitment in many people.

Moving away from the baseball analogy, we need to recognize that although insight and response are necessary for faith, they are not sufficient. In other words, there are cases of insight and response that do not amount to faith, for example when a doctor intuits a diagnosis and takes action to effect a cure. Because we cannot specify sufficient conditions, we do not have a perfect definition of faith. We can identify faith, and we can often say what faith is not, but we cannot fully say what faith is.

The faith of any individual is uncertain; there is no faith without doubt. Thus Francis Spufford says, "The life of faith has just as many he-doesn't-exist-the-bastard moments as the life of disbelief. Probably more of them, if anything, given that we believers tend to return to the subject more often, producing many more opportunities to be disappointed."[17] At its best, faith is characterized by both passion and humility, a sense that one understands enough to take action but not enough to be infallible in one's beliefs or actions. Faith is not foolishness or gullibility—those exist in abundance in the religious realm, but they are not faith. Thomas Merton says, "Faith is not blind conformity to a prejudice—a prejudgment. It is a decision, a judgment that is fully and deliberately taken in the light of a truth that cannot be proven. It is not merely the acceptance of a decision that has been made by somebody else."[18] Despite being shared with others, faith is a profoundly individual matter. It is perhaps like the feeling that some characters in *The Matrix* have, "a splinter in your mind, driving you mad"—directing you to look beyond physical reality for something more. We can reason about it, but it is not ultimately a matter of reason. As Tim Crane says, "Faith is not certainty but something more like a committed struggle to understand in the face of the palpable mystery of the world."[19]

The guiding mantra of medieval philosophy was "faith seeking understanding." Faith comes first according to this formula. One believes on faith, for example, that God exists, and then one uses the tools of reason to confirm what one believes on faith. Thus, Thomas Aquinas offered his famous Five Ways, his five arguments for the existence of God. These arguments have been the object of debate and discussion ever since Aquinas offered them. People of faith tend to find them highly convincing, and people who lack faith often find them full of holes. It's unlikely that a single atheist has ever been moved to belief in God by reading and contemplating the Five Ways, at least not belief in the Judeo-Christian God. That's the funny thing about the Five Ways: at best they establish the existence of a creator; they do not establish the existence of the Judeo-Christian God. As Aquinas saw it, reason cannot prove the existence of the Judeo-Christian God in all of his particulars. Faith is required for that; faith takes us the rest of the way.

We need to pay attention to lived experience, the life of the heart, and not just abstract thought, the life of the mind. Where lived experience contrasts with abstract thought and there is no empirical evidence that fully settles the matter, we can, and perhaps should, prefer the lived experience. This is the view that Miguel de Unamuno offers in his *Tragic Sense of Life*. As he puts it, "Reason and faith are two enemies, neither of which can maintain itself without the other."[20] Most Christian philosophers have sought to eliminate, or at least minimize, conflict between faith and reason, but Unamuno is an exception. Seeing life without faith as bloodless and life without reason as foolish, he did not attempt to reconcile the life of the heart and the life of the mind. Indeed, it was their very conflict that made life worth living, as he saw it. "For my part I do not wish to make peace between my heart and my head, between my faith and my reason—I wish rather that there should be war between them!"[21] Despite the war between faith and reason, though, Unamuno ultimately prefers faith, saying that "Life cannot submit itself to reason, because the end of life is living and not understanding."[22]

In contrast to Unamuno, who saw faith and reason in conflict, Augustine saw them in cooperation. Faith, though, is primary for Augustine. Indeed, he says, "Understanding is the recompense of faith. Therefore, seek not to understand so that you believe, but believe so that you may understand, for 'unless you believe, you will not understand.'"[23] If we have faith, reason can help us to see the ways that many features of the natural world that appear to be imperfect are actually part of a greater plan and perfection. Augustine advised, though, that in places where reason did not detect the greater plan and perfection we should have faith. As Hebrews 11:1 says, "Faith is the assurance of things hoped for, the conviction of things not seen." The ideal is that faith and reason should be mutually reinforcing. Reason can often bolster faith, and faith can lead us to look in the right places for reason that supports it. To this day, the *Catechism of the Catholic Church* says, "Though faith is above reason, there can never be any real discrepancy between faith and reason. Since the same God who reveals mysteries and infuses faith has bestowed reason on the human mind, God can never deny himself, nor can truth ever contradict truth."[24]

In the Augustinian spirit, the philosopher Jean-Luc Marion speaks of faith in terms of belief, arguing that in some matters of faith we must believe first in order to understand. As he says, "And one only has it available if one reaches it as it gives itself, namely by faith. In order to see, one must believe, but by believing one only accomplishes a work of reason."[25] By way of illustration, Marion discusses the disciples on the road to Emmaus who do not recognize the risen Christ (Luke 24:13–25). They do not believe and so are unable to see, to see what is obvious. They do not believe someone could rise from the dead, and thus they can't see that this is the risen Christ with them.[26] Marion's argument is that, like the disciples on the road to Emmaus, we fail to believe our eyes. The evidence is there. Faith does not fill in the gaps, but opens our eyes: "What we lack in order to believe is quite simply one with what we lack in order to see. Faith does not compensate, either here or anywhere else, for a defect of visibility: on the contrary, it allows reception of the understanding of the phenomenon and the strength to bear the glare of its brilliance. Faith does not manage the deficit of evidence—it alone renders the gaze apt to see the excess of the preeminent saturated phenomenon, the Revelation."[27]

In folksy terms, we can understand Marion's philosophy of "believing in order to see" as illustrated by the figure-ground phenomenon of coming to see the name Jesus written in the negative space in a sign. We are accustomed to reading dark letters on a light background. The negative space gestalt reverses things, and so we are at first unable to see that anything is written there. Only by believing, usually because of the testimony of others, that the name Jesus is written on the sign do we make the effort to adjust our eyes and focus to see what is there, the name Jesus written in light letters on a dark background.

In contrast to Marion, who sees faith as rational, Kierkegaard sees faith as going beyond reason, taking us where reason cannot reach. Faith does not culminate in rational understanding. Rather, echoing Pascal, Kierkegaard says that "faith begins precisely where thought stops."[28] Human reason, much like human sight, speed, and speech, is limited. It will take you only so far. To go the rest of the way requires a leap of faith. It is as if reason will take you to the edge of a precipice and faith is required to make the leap over the chasm to the other side. You can stay where you are or you can risk the leap, which could fall short and leave you at the bottom of the abyss, or which could succeed and land you on the other side. The catch is that you cannot really see the other side from where you are. It is unknown and unfamiliar. By contrast, your starting place is familiar and perhaps comfortable. Kierkegaard thus characterizes the leap of faith as being made in the midst of "fear and trembling." The leap is not made out of a sense of certainty, but rather in great doubt because it involves tremendous risk.

Kierkegaard takes Abraham as his ideal of faith, specifically Abraham's faithful willingness to follow God's command to sacrifice his son Isaac. Dread is left out of the details of the Biblical account, but, according to Kierkegaard, Abraham would have felt great dread. Of course he did not want to sacrifice his son Isaac, miraculously born to his wife Sarah in her old age. Abraham loved Isaac and saw him as part of the fulfillment of God's promise to give him more descendants than could be counted. Chronologically, the story takes place before God gives the Ten Commandments to Moses, but Abraham wouldn't have needed stone tablets to know that killing an innocent person is wrong, especially his own son. So when Abraham heard the voice telling him to sacrifice Isaac, he could not have been certain that it was the voice of God. Reason unaided by faith would have suggested that it was anything but the voice of God making this request. But Abraham had faith, indeed took the leap of faith, and he was paradoxically rewarded when God provided a ram for the sacrifice at the last moment.

As if in reply to Kierkegaard's claim that "faith begins precisely where thought stops," Nietzsche quips, "Faith means not wanting to know what is true."[29] Nietzsche seems to admonish us: keep thinking and don't put your head in the sand. His advice is tough, not tender. But Kierkegaard's Abraham does not play ostrich and deny obvious truth. Rather, he dwells in the midst of uncertainty and passion brought on by flirtation with an absurd belief: that God is speaking directly to him and telling him to kill his innocent, beloved son. Kierkegaard's Abraham seems to display admirable courage. But Nietzsche's words resound. Not wanting to know what is true can be dangerous when it comes to religion. Commenting on Kierkegaard's valorization of Abraham, the Nietzsche scholar Walter Kaufmann says, "Far from being unfortunately rare in our time, such blind fanaticism is one of the scourges of humanity. There are too many men, not too few, who are willing to believe that it is their sacred duty to sacrifice others."[30] Kaufmann's words have proven prophetic, as reports of suicide bombers have become ordinary news. Surely the faith of such extremists is misplaced. A similar problem is to be found with Marion's "believing in order to see." Namely, you may end up seeing what is not really there. We all need to guard against wishful thinking and confirmation bias, but "believing in order to see" simply invites them. What's more, "believing in order to see" will lead to contradictory results with, for example, Christians and Muslims coming to see incompatible things.

Martin Luther claimed that reason is a whore. A philosopher, a skeptic, can argue both sides of a question, sometimes both equally effectively. For Luther, only faith will tell us what is true. But one may respond to Luther that "faith is a whore." People have strong, genuine, sincere faith in contradictory things—and in awful things. The faith of suicide bombers is no less real than the faith of saintly humanitarians. So faith by itself cannot tell us what is true, and faith may lead us astray. Faith may be a gift. But, as the atheist scientist Jerry Coyne points out, the German word *Gift* means poison.[31] So what kind of gift is faith? Is it a divine present, or a man-made poison? Is faith a natural yearning or an artificial creation?

For many people, faith is bound up with "the purpose-driven life." As Smith says, "faith differs from un-faith in seeing that life and the universe do, indeed, have a point—a cosmic point; and that man can be grasped by it, and be transported."[32] A person without faith is at a disadvantage in not seeing a pre-given purpose to his life and his world. The person of faith, by contrast, has the comfort of thinking that no matter how badly things may be going in the moment, God has a plan for each person's life and for the world. Let's face it, though, the world is a mess, and human existence is fraught with anxiety. As the Christian psychologist Richard Beck puts it, "Life is experienced as broken glass. Life is experienced as shattered. The puzzle pieces here are shards, bits of brokenness that we try to piece together again into a whole. And as we handle the pieces, we are often cut and wounded. Life resists our attempts at putting the pieces together, intellectually and emotionally."[33]

We may be tempted to think that faith is indeed "not wanting to know what is true," a defense mechanism for dealing with a difficult world in which life has no ultimate purpose. Along these lines, Sam Harris says that "Religious faith is simply *unjustified* belief in matters of ultimate concern—specifically in propositions that promise some mechanism by which human life can be spared the ravages of time and death."[34] Perhaps this is right. Faith can be a defense mechanism and a source of false comfort. We may wonder what authentic faith would look like. Indeed, Abraham Joshua Heschel says we are "in greater need of a proof for the authenticity of faith than of a proof for the existence of God."[35]

Taking up Heschel's challenge, Beck concedes that faith can be an inauthentic defense mechanism, but nonetheless argues that "Faith does not necessarily imply a defensive theology. Faith oftentimes expresses the exact opposite, the admission that life is disordered and that the believer is adrift in a hostile cosmos. This is the faith experience of the lament, the cry of the winter believer, the sick soul. Faith exists but it is *not* being used to repress existential anxiety."[36] Beck's mention of the "sick soul" is a reference to William James, who distinguishes between the healthy-minded individual and the sick soul in *The Varieties of Religious Experience*. Whereas the healthy-minded individual is free of doubt and comforted by his faith, the sick soul "acknowledges negativity, that embraces doubt, and that is honest about its experience of god-forsakenness. And yet these experiences are not symptoms of unfaith but rather acts of 'bold faith.'"[37] Despite the negative connotation, the "sick soul" is really the healthier of the two. The sick soul has the more authentic experience of suffering and doubt that comes with mature and sincere faith. Mother Teresa fits the description, and indeed, James himself seems to have been a "sick soul." Most likely, though, he was some hybrid of the two. I suspect that the healthy-minded and the sick soul are not pure types, especially the sick soul. The typical sick soul probably takes some existential consolation in his faith. He just doesn't take it to the extreme of illusion and delusion that the healthy-minded does.

Contra Sam Harris and others, some faith is authentic. Clearly, though, most people do not have authentic faith, not even most religious believers. And even those with authentic faith may be badly misguided, as in the case of suicide bombers. Let's return to Sol from *Crimes and Misdemeanors*. If his faith is authentic, perhaps it is a gift. If it is a divine present, though, why is faith given so strongly to some and perhaps not at all to others? Is it a matter of grace, an undeserved gift that no one has a right to complain about not getting? Alternatively, the philosopher Alvin Plantinga claims that the *sensus divinitatis* is broken by the effects of sin.[38] Perhaps, though, faith needs a verb form for us to make sense of it. "To faith" is both active and passive. It is like trying to tune in a radio signal. One must actively search for the signal and tune it in, but one must also passively receive the signal. One does not determine the contents of the signal; one only receives it. And the signal once found is not guaranteed to stay. As time passes, it may take additional tuning and adjustment to receive the signal. Ultimately the signal we receive is processed only imperfectly. As Paul says, we see through a glass, darkly (1 Corinthians

13:12). Insight can be partial and imperfect and yet still lead to good response or action.

Faith seems more like a man-made poison when we consider suicide bombers or members of the church of Christian Science, who do not treat illnesses with modern medicine. This might just seem to be foolishness on the level of snake handlers who believe they will be safe from venom as long as they have faith. But snake handlers don't force anyone to follow their beliefs, especially not children. By contrast, Christian Scientists refuse medical care for their children. Such people have insight and take action, but the results are often disastrous, and not just for themselves. Yet their faith is authentic. Christian Scientists, like snake handlers, can point to scripture for the basis of their faith, and obviously they feel it is true. Unlike many typical Christians, they are ready and willing to take major risks on the basis of their faith. Beyond their scriptural justification, snake handlers and Christian Scientists can feel the truth of their beliefs. But is this a matter of genuine insight leading to action? Or is it a misplaced reliance on the heart rather than the head?

Stephen Colbert famously introduced the word "truthiness" into the lexicon, meaning a kind of intuitive or gut-level claim to knowledge that ignores or flies in the face of evidence. Colbert coined the term in response to George W. Bush, who seemed to trust his gut more than facts when it came to making major political decisions. Obviously, "truthiness" is a term of derision, and it would seem to apply to matters of faith. Snake handlers and Christian Scientists take extreme actions based on faith, but even mainstream Christians require faith that seems to amount to truthiness. The cosmologist Carl Sagan was fond of saying that "extraordinary claims require extraordinary evidence." That Jesus was the son of God and born of a virgin, that he died for our sins and rose from the dead: these are extraordinary claims that lack extraordinary evidence. But it is ultimately faith rather than evidence that is offered as the justification for belief in these claims. What would Colbert say? The man who coined that term "truthiness" is a devout Catholic. So presumably he thinks that charges of truthiness do not apply in this realm.

Because educated and intelligent adults claim an experience of faith we have reason to take the claim seriously, but not necessarily to accept their claim as valid. Carl Sagan, an agnostic, gives the example of the invisible dragon in his garage.[39] Because it's invisible you can't see the dragon. It floats, so you can't see footprints. Its fire isn't hot, so you can't feel its breath. There could still be a flying invisible dragon in the garage, but a reasonable person hasn't been given proper evidence to take the claim seriously. "Pastafarians" will note the similarity to their favorite satirical deity, the Flying Spaghetti Monster, who likewise eludes all attempts to detect it. The dragon in the garage and the Flying Spaghetti Monster are unfalsifiable hypotheses; believers will not accept any evidence as counting against them. In the minds of believers, there is nothing that would ever disprove the existence of the Flying Spaghetti Monster.[40] The scientist is rightly frustrated by this stance. At a certain point, a search needs to be considered a fruitless search; nothing has been found because most likely nothing is there.

Sometimes, though, strange claims turn out to have some basis in reality. Sometimes they're even completely accurate. Despite the initial disbelief of Europeans, there really is a venomous, duck-billed, egg-laying mammal. Every schoolchild now knows that it's called a platypus. It took Europeans until 1901 to accept the existence of the okapi, which bears zebra-like stripes on parts of its body, resembles a donkey, and is most closely related to the giraffe. Rumors of apelike creatures are common in various parts of the world. Hoaxes have been responsible for many of the rumors, but it turns out that some of the people who claim to have seen the Yeti in the Himalayas saw something, just not what they thought they saw. DNA gathered from hair samples suggests the creature is a polar bear that mated with a brown bear, perhaps a hybrid or perhaps a previously unknown species.[41] So, it is worth asking the question of what people are sensing or detecting even if the answer turns out to be something other than what they thought. Clearly, investigations need to continue before conclusions can be drawn. Extraordinary claims require extraordinary evidence, but, as Jerry Coyne likes to add, "we can never say such evidence is impossible."[42]

Faith in God may be merely wishful thinking or even delusion, collective or individual. We can never have absolute proof and thus absolute certainty one way or another. For that matter, scientists must admit that there is no scientific proof for the belief that all of reality is physical; nor is there scientific proof for the reliability of mathematics, logic, or induction. These bases of scientific reasoning are not matters of faith, but they are not beyond doubt. Indeed, it is part of the human condition to be stuck with a degree of doubt and uncertainty. Our beliefs exist along a continuum of certainty, and where they fall on that continuum will be determined by both objective and subjective factors. The same reasons and evidence may result in beliefs that occupy different locations on the continuum for different people, and even for the same person over the course of time. Still, we need to take action even in the midst of uncertainty. As a standard, Coyne suggests asking yourself this question: Is there enough proof that you would be willing to bet your savings on it?[43] When it comes to God, not all intelligent, informed, and honest people will answer the same way. We must, therefore, be tolerant and humble in the face of differing conclusions.

6

A CIVIL DISCOURSE

Intellectual humility is both a starting point and a goal. Recognizing that I don't know everything, I need to begin a conversation with the sense that I could be wrong and that there is much to learn. Because my discussion partner may not manifest the same intellectual humility, there is a temptation to withdraw it on my part. So it becomes a challenge to maintain intellectual humility and preserve it by the end of the discussion. Consider a discussion with a child. One may begin with the fine intentions of admitting and displaying one's lack of complete knowledge, but the child may say and do things that make it difficult to maintain that humility. Adults are even more challenging than children in that regard, because they should behave better. One can easily see the value of maintaining one's intellectual humility in discussion with a child, but one can easily lose sight of that value in discussion with an adult. This is not to suggest that one should think of the adult as a child, but that one should realize the greater difficulty in conversing with an adult. One should thus mindfully maintain the goal of preserving intellectual humility.

Genuine intellectual humility is closely tied to intellectual honesty, which requires that one be self-reflective about the basis for accepting beliefs, views, and positions. There is a great temptation to start with a position that one wants to accept—whether on the basis of comfort, tradition, inertia, self-interest, or some other motivation—

and find reasons to justify it. The problem gets compounded when one either doesn't realize, or just loses sight of the fact that, this is what one is doing. To an extent this is common, maybe even universal.

The physicist Richard Feynman captures this in a certain way when he says, "You must not fool yourself—and you are the easiest person to fool."[1] It is easy for a scientist to fall in love with her own hypothesis or pet theory and then to look only for evidence that confirms it. We are all liable to this tendency, known as confirmation bias. The dishonesty involved is not plagiarism or fraud; it is self-deception. Experience confirms that it is easier to fool yourself than anyone else, but there is a puzzle at the heart of that deception. Lying to or deceiving someone else is straightforward: you convince them that what is false is actually true. This can work if they don't know the truth. But in lying to yourself, you are somehow convincing yourself that what you know to be false is actually true. This is like playing hide-and-seek with yourself—it shouldn't work. But in this case it does work—we fool ourselves, and we do it by directing our attention to reasons and evidence that confirm our beliefs and away from reasons and evidence that disconfirm them.

I myself am the easiest person to fool because no one wants to believe my theory more than I do. Others may be willing to be convinced, but I myself have my ego invested in being right. Of course, all of this goes not just for scientific theories, but for philosophical, religious, and political views too. I want to be right, and I'm not above lying to myself in order to be right. So intellectual honesty is not an easy virtue to achieve; we seem inclined against it. Left all on my own, or even in the company of like-minded peers, my level of intellectual honesty is likely to be low, no matter how great my dedication to truth. We need others to help us develop intellectual honesty. Because I am myself the easiest person to fool, I need others around me. They are less likely to be fooled and more likely to put me in my place. Particularly important, then, are people who are inclined to disagree with me and challenge me.

Unfortunately, we tend to surround ourselves with like-minded people who aid us in our self-deception. Thankfully, though, it is difficult for us to be fully successful in bubbling ourselves in this way. True friends want what is best for one another and challenge one another to improve and be their best. Often this takes the form of practical moral improvement, but it can and should take the form of improvement in intellectual honesty as well. To be a good friend, then, requires that I be willing to tell uncomfortable truths and to challenge my friend in ways that create tension. This is not just part of being a good friend, but also part of being a good peer, relative, colleague, or citizen. We have a responsibility to one another to prod, poke, and play gadfly. This, however, is a difficult task to get right. Indeed, it cost Socrates his life. On the one hand we need to mind our own business, but on the other hand what someone else thinks may be everyone's business to the extent that it manifests in public actions. So, for example, it is one thing for a person to think that his religion offers the only path to salvation, but it is another thing for a person to think that anyone who does not accept his religion should be imprisoned or executed.

Socrates saw smug self-contentment and pursuit of material success as detrimental to the life and future of Athens, and so he set out to expose the ignorance and self-deception of the Athenians, including many leading citizens. Predictably, this was not appreciated by those he exposed. Despite the fact that he claimed to know nothing, Socrates came across as a know-it-all. No doubt, he was a bit of a jerk, but his execution made him a martyr for the philosophic quest. He has been imitated countless times ever since by much bigger jerks.

It is tempting to take Socrates as a role model, but unless one wants to become a martyr for a cause, it is not wise. And if one wants to become a martyr for a cause, one must ask oneself why. Very few causes ever require or even benefit from martyrs. Martyrs tend to be sanctimonious and ineffective. Far better is to play gadfly with the kind of openness and intellectual humility that Socrates often lacked. For all his professions of ignorance, Socrates seemed to have a secret pride in his realization that he knew nothing, and this pride is the enemy of true intellectual humility. Socrates claimed that the oracle at Delphi had said that no one was wiser than Socrates, and so he had set out to disprove the literal sense of the oracle by finding someone who was wiser. Ironically, the oracle was confirmed for Socrates in his realization that by admitting his own ignorance he was wiser than all others. The god Apollo was believed to speak through the oracle at Delphi, and so Socrates saw himself as a man on a mission. Practically nothing is more dangerous; all kinds of things seem justifiable to a man on a mission.

Socrates's tone may have been among the first casualties of his mission. Despite his professed humility, Socrates often did not come across as genuinely humble, and his evangelism for skepticism was often aggressive. He should have realized that not everyone was buying what he was selling; not everyone hooked up to the Matrix is ready to be unplugged. It is not easy to play the role of gadfly if you want to get it right. You must first have intellectual humility yourself and make a point of highlighting your own faults and shortcomings. Recognizing your own imperfection, you must have sympathy for imperfection in others. The goal is to cultivate genuine openness in oneself and others, not to replace one certainty with another.

It may sound like I'm preaching and maybe even being hypocritical when it comes to intellectual humility and intellectual honesty. That is the risk I take by bringing up the subject and thereby implicitly offering myself as an example. Let me hasten to add that I am a flawed, imperfect example. Nonetheless I have sincerely tried to practice intellectual humility by remaining open to correction and change of mind. In fact, I have sought it out by discussing the ideas in this book and sharing earlier drafts of this book with people who disagree with me in a variety of ways. I have benefited from feedback and criticism given by atheists, agnostics, and believers alike. And I remain open to correction and change of mind. This book is not the last word for me; it is a snapshot that captures a moment in time. It is a catalyst for further thought for me and hopefully for the reader. And I would be glad to hear from readers to continue the ongoing dialogue on the topics this book discusses.

It is important not to presume agreement, especially concerning religion. I was guilty of this in my original *New York Times* article in which I simply presumed that atheists would agree that they occasionally have their doubts. I have since learned that some atheists claim never to doubt their unbelief. And, what's more, many of them resent my suggestion that they should. Previous chapters articulate what I mean by "God" and "doubt" when I say that "any honest atheist must admit that she has her doubts." But without those nuanced explanations, my statement was inadvertently inflammatory.

There is a suspicion of nuance among some people, as if by making distinctions one is weaseling out of truth. Actually, reality and the consideration of it is complex, such that it requires nuance. Likewise, there is an intolerance for ambiguity. People want certainty and clarity, rightly so. But not all issues permit or deliver the level of certainty and clarity sought. In such cases, the proper response is not to take comfort in faux certainty, but to dance with the ambiguity. Socrates held that the unexamined life is not worth living. In part this means that we should not treat our beliefs as ever so fully settled that they are beyond all doubt and the possibility of reconsideration. I take this to be true for all people. It does not surprise me when religious extremists reject it, but it does surprise and sadden me when some atheists reject it.

We face the question of how best to understand and communicate with people who disagree with us. In understanding, it is appropriate to apply the principle of charity, whereby we attribute the most favorable and reasonable interpretation to the words and intentions of others. In communicating about others who disagree with us, we need to avoid straw man and ad hominem fallacies, and in speaking with them we need to listen actively and sympathetically. We can learn from people we think are wrong, and we can respect them. As Tim Crane says, "Tolerance does not require respect for the views one is tolerating. But it does go hand in hand with respect for people as autonomous individuals."[2]

We need to avoid getting bubbled in, such that we talk only with those in general agreement with us. Much better is to spend time with and among people who do not agree with us on a host of issues. Not only does this open our eyes, but it sharpens our minds so that we can understand our own views and arguments better. The philosopher John Stuart Mill argues that we need to learn the other side of the argument at least as well as our own, if not better. If we know only our own side, then we don't even know that.[3] Minority opinion is valuable, and so we need to create not just the legal right for its expression but the civil atmosphere in which it can be comfortably expressed. The minority opinion may turn out to be right. But even if the minority opinion turns out to be wrong, we benefit from engaging with it. Such engagement forces us to examine our own views much more carefully, and it saves them from becoming "dead dogma."[4] It is also possible, and maybe even likely, that the truth lies somewhere in between the majority and minority views. So we need to be quick to see where people we disagree with are right, even partially.

Mill highlights the importance of learning minority or opposing views from their sources. It is not enough to get a convenient summary of them from someone who disagrees with them.[5] Even if such a source does their best to be fair and objective in their presentation, they are unlikely to be completely fair and objective. They are also unlikely to be able to answer questions and challenges satisfactorily on behalf of the views they oppose. Knowing the other side is more than just being able to pass a test in which you name the views and reasons for the views held by the other side. It also involves having an appreciation for the feelings that motivate the other side.

Can one pass the "Ideological Turing Test"?[6] The original Turing Test is a supposed way of determining whether a computer is intelligent or aware or conscious. Can the computer answer questions in such a way that a person asking them via computer cannot guess successfully who is answering, a human or an unaided computer? To pass the Ideological Turing Test one must be able to present the other side's views in such a way that people cannot tell whether those are your own views or not. This involves not just being accurate and being able to answer questions, but tapping into the feelings behind the views such that one articulates them with the characteristic tone and feeling.

So, for example, in the realm of American politics, progressives should watch Fox News, and conservatives should watch MSNBC to learn the views of the opposing side from the source. Part of the difficulty in listening to the other side is tolerating tone. For many progressives the tone of Fox News will be so obnoxious as to make listening to it with an open mind very difficult. And the same goes for conservatives attempting to watch MSNBC. These outlets have tones that particularly appeal to their viewers, making them feel confirmed in their views and their righteousness. The use of such tones makes sense for the purposes of attracting viewers and selling advertising, but it is not good for the larger discourse. Interpersonal discourse can and should strive to do better than this.

Comedy such as *The Daily Show* is a bad source for news and opinion. The viewer can gather many of the basic facts of a story or view by watching a parody or sketch, but the tone delivers a message concerning what view a smart person should have about the facts. This is commonly accomplished with a straw man, setting up the opposing side or opposing view to appear stupid or heartless by tweaking the presentation for comedic effect, such as taking a quote out of context or not giving the full context of why a view is held. A straw man can be a hilarious caricature that highlights a feature that may otherwise go undetected. Indeed, there is often insight and value in such caricatures, but there is a problem when such caricatures crowd out other images. Of course there is a perfectly understandable motivation for producing such caricatures: people like them. They attract viewers, sell newspapers, etc. No one should stop producing them. The obligation is on the side of the consumer, though, to ask himself whether he is consuming or being consumed by such images.

The audience generally realizes and gives itself credit for knowing when a straw man is being offered for comedic effect, but not always. In the realm of religion, the most bigoted and simplistic religious believers are often presented as representative of all believers. Likewise, angry, obnoxious atheists are the stand-in for all atheists. There are plenty of bigoted religious fools, just as there are plenty of angry, obnoxious atheists. Such people harm their own cause, but it is incumbent upon us to look for the very best representatives of views that oppose our own—sincere and intelligent people. The other side cannot be dismissed with a laugh or the wave of a hand. Because tone is infectious, we need to avoid listening, watching, and reading sources that agree with us in a smug, nasty, or condescending tone. It is tempting to go to such sources for affirmation, but they are poisonous and ruinous of productive discourse.

Words matter. We are not purely rational and logical creatures; we have emotional responses to words and their connotations. Some words can be unintentionally inflammatory. When I wrote in the *New York Times* that any honest atheist must admit that he sometimes has his doubts, I did not intend to call anyone dishonest. I wasn't imagining that a large number of atheists do not think of themselves as having any doubts and that they would take me to be calling them dishonest. But that is what happened. Similar problems can result from the careless use of words like "logical," "rational," and "intelligent" when the implication is that someone who disagrees is illogical, irrational, or unintelligent.

Too often in debate and discussion we use the rhetoric of war. We think of ourselves as engaged in intellectual combat using weapons against an enemy or rival. We speak of winning or losing, of crushing or defeating an opponent. [7] There is a satisfaction taken in winning that is particularly misplaced and misguided because all things must remain open to debate; the case is never really fully closed. It would be better to use the rhetoric of diplomacy. Sometimes such word choices seem namby-pamby and overly careful, but really they are a mark of strength and restraint. It is easier to be uncensored and just say whatever comes to one's mind. The rhetoric of diplomacy is a delicate instrument that works over time on the emotional level as well as the rational level. It sends the message to the other side that they are respected and that they are heard. And this makes the other side more likely to listen.

There has been an unfortunate tendency on some college campuses to shut down and shout down speakers whom students and faculty regard as wrong. To be clear, this is not a violation of the First Amendment. No speaker has the particular right to speak on a particular college campus at a particular time and on a particular date. The speaker simply has the right to express his or her views without government censorship, and no one is denying that right. So, students and faculty who shut down or shout down speakers do nothing illegal, but they do harm themselves by denying themselves the opportunity to engage with people on the other side of issues. They also develop a bad habit of demonizing those they disagree with. This can lead to ad hominem arguments, whereby they dismiss anything that is said by a certain person, just because that person said it. Of course, we often need to consider the source in deciding how seriously to take a certain claim, but we should ultimately consider the claim on its own merits.

We must be careful not to see others as dangerous when they are not. Yes, there are dangerous religious zealots who are ready, willing, and able to kill those who disagree with them. But such people constitute a small minority of religious believers or adherents to any particular faith. Likewise, there have been atheists such as Stalin and Mao who have committed atrocities, justified by their political philosophies and fearing no divine retribution. We need to be careful of guilt by association, though. Such people exist at the extremes, and there is a whole spectrum occupied by believers and atheists alike, from completely benign to terribly dangerous. It does no good to think of all religious believers or all adherents to a certain religion as dangerous; nor does it do any good to think of all atheists as dangerous. Notice here that I am speaking of how we think of such people. It is not just a matter of what we say or write, but what we think, because what we think impacts our actions and subtly influences the tone of what we say and write. It may be difficult to completely free ourselves of all prejudgments about religious believers or atheists (or agnostics), but we can at least be aware of our tendency to make prejudgments and try to catch ourselves and correct ourselves in the act of prejudgment. Part of the problem with such prejudgment is that it treats an individual merely as a member of a group. It is often helpful to begin by recognizing that a person is a member of a particular group, but more is required in order to see the person for who they really are. One must look to see the ways in which the individual differs from the group and from one's assessment of the group. This is not simply a principle of morality; it is a principle of effective communication. It is in one's own interest to practice the principle, and it would foster civility if everyone did.

What is civility? In a word it is respect. It involves manners and decorum, the little rituals that signal to others that their views are heard and taken seriously. Repeating another person's views back to them and asking for confirmation of accuracy is a sign of civility and appreciation. This is the opposite of the way uncivil discussion commonly proceeds, with one side listening to the other with suspicion in order to pick out some small part of what they say in order to exploit it. This may amount to taking a quote out of context or drawing an unintended consequence or conclusion from what is said. It is a matter of scoring points in a debate rather than arriving at mutual understanding. Of course, there is nothing wrong with wanting to win a debate, but it is possible to win a debate and lose the chance to change anyone's mind. When the exchange of ideas is nasty and uncivil, people watching or involved in the exchange double down on the views they already had, even if those ideas fare poorly in the debate.

Listening carefully is hard work. It seems to be a lost art, though it may never have been common. There may never have been an Eden in which people listened carefully to one another. Often, listening takes the form of scanning the text of another's words, written or spoken, for some point to seize on, a mistake or "gotcha moment." It is understandable why politicians and their surrogates do this: it is part of the game they play. But we do ourselves a disservice when we imitate that game. Our goal should be to seek the truth, not to defend or advance an agenda. Too often, listening takes the form of waiting with pretend patience for the gap in the conversation where one can jump in with one's own view. All the while, the pretend listener is rehearsing his lines in his head, hearing less and less of what is being said. The desire for a clever retort overrides the desire for correct understanding, and the result is sham dialogue, political theater rather than a meeting of the minds. Many people think that listening amounts to letting the other person talk while calculating a response or even an intellectual takedown. This is not listening; it is barely even hearing. This is not seeking first to understand; it is making sure that one gets one's own words in and points across. It is obvious when the other person in a discussion is "listening" in this way. Their eyes and body language make it apparent, as does their abrupt interjection when they sense an opening. And this often leads to a vicious cycle in which the other person senses he has not been listened to, feels disrespected, and reacts by returning the treatment.

The Prayer of St. Francis urges us to seek first to understand and then to be understood. From a certain perspective, this may seem weak and ineffective, but nothing could be further from the truth. Seeking first to understand projects strength.[8] One is secure enough and open-minded enough to fully consider what the other person has to say, to listen to it not just for the reasons, but for the emotions, behind it. Demonstration of such understanding is displayed in repeating the view back to the speaker and asking for confirmation and in asking questions that demonstrate a desire to know rather than a desire to dissect. In person, such listening manifests itself in sustained eye contact and open body language. The encounter can be exhausting and draining, but that is better than the feelings of anger, frustration, and self-righteousness that often result from disputes and debates.

Oscar Wilde is reputed to have said, "A gentleman is one who never hurts anyone's feelings unintentionally."[9] By that strict standard, I am not a gentleman, but I try to be. I have people in my life who hurt my feelings unintentionally on a regular basis. Some of them, sometimes, should know better. They are culpably ignorant in the way Wilde's formula suggests. Other times, of course, they are just human, and because they are not all-knowing they cannot avoid hurting my feelings. Sex, politics, and religion are often regarded as discussion topics to be avoided. Certainly, when we don't know a person well this avoidance is a good policy, but since these are among the most interesting and vital concerns for most people, we are not inclined to avoid the topics altogether. While we may not raise the topics for discussion at the extended-family gathering for Thanksgiving dinner, we will raise them with people whose views we presume are like our own. And this is where we court less obvious trouble. By discussing such topics with people who agree with us, we risk getting bubbled in and thinking that all reasonable people agree with us. We also risk violating Wilde's dictum. This is particularly offensive when it is presumed that the person addressed must agree with you because they are like you in some other way. Regrettably, my experience has been that professors are particularly prone to this. In a way, this is understandable because academic culture is so monolithic, but for that reason it is all the more disturbing. Those who are educating the youth are often bubbled in to the extent that they can't even conceive of honest disagreement on issues that matter.

Of course, part of the point of Wilde's quip is that if he has insulted you, he has done it on purpose. I have experienced plenty of insults from non-gentlemen but also plenty from gentlemen who feel obliged to needle me. I almost always appreciate honest disagreement and invitation to discuss and debate. But sometimes this needling takes the form of people pretending to have forgotten that we disagree; they pretend not to realize that their presumption of agreement on some issue is obnoxious to me. I understand and appreciate the rhetorical force and effect of such sophisticated needling, but I find it distasteful nonetheless. It has the feel of trying to coerce conformity through presumed consensus. Rather than offer an argument for a position, it appeals to the group or to authority to suggest that if I disagree then I should reconsider. In fact, the suggestion seems to be that I should change my mind about my conclusion and eventually I will see the wisdom of the reasons for that new conclusion.

A friend of mine who faces similar pressures and tactics describes his survival strategy as like that of the survivors on *The Walking Dead*, who sometimes strategically smear themselves with zombie guts to avoid detection by the zombies. I have to confess that I have done this myself, pretended to believe what I don't in order to avoid the hassle.

Like the academic world, the world of twelve-step recovery tends to make marginalizing presumptions. Belief in a "higher power" is a major element of twelve-step recovery. A higher power need not be God, certainly not any particular conception of God. It is even suggested that one can make one's group one's higher power—but that is generally suggested as a transitional step. The book *Alco-*

holics Anonymous serves as the basic text of twelve-step recovery and contains the chapter "To the Agnostic," the basic message of which is that it is all right to start out as an agnostic or even an atheist, but that won't last long.

Faith in a higher power has helped millions of people in their recoveries, but one has to wonder how many more people have failed in their recoveries because they were not able to cultivate the requisite faith in God as a higher power. While much of the rhetoric in recovery groups is broad and inclusive enough to make room for agnostics and atheists, even more of the rhetoric makes it difficult for nonbelievers to feel accepted and to feel like they are doing a good job of practicing the program of recovery. As a result, many smear the zombie guts of belief on themselves.

No matter where we find ourselves, we hope for the possibility of open and honest dialogue. When we fail to respect minority opinions, we all lose.

7

THE PHYSICIST'S HORSESHOE
AND THE ATHEIST'S PRAYER

Legend has it that the physicist Niels Bohr had a horseshoe hanging above his door. A colleague asked him why, to which he responded, "It's for luck." The colleague then asked him if he believed in luck. Bohr reassured him that as a scientist he did not believe in luck. Puzzled, the colleague asked again why Bohr had the horseshoe hanging above his door. Bohr responded, "I'm told that you don't have to believe in order for it to work." We can draw a lesson here about prayer. It has been said that nothing fails like prayer, and that may be true. So what could be the point of prayer, especially for an atheist? In a sense, prayer can work particularly well for an atheist because she has no expectation of divine intervention.[1] Prayer does not change the world for me, but it can change me for the world.[2]

Some atheists like Sam Harris advocate the benefits of meditation, stripped of its religious baggage. But meditation is only half the picture. Meditation typically requires silence whereas prayer requires speech. Prayer too can be stripped of its religious baggage and preserved for its practical benefits. As we'll see, the chief benefits of prayer are the expressions of gratitude, humility, and hope. Prayer does not need to be directed at a deity. Rather, it can be directed at the universe. One can express gratitude in the abstract, humility in one's small place, and hope for the future.[3] Instead of seeing such prayer as an unfortunate relic from a religious past, one can see it as a valuable ritual in which one pauses to get proper perspective.

Is prayer for an atheist any more contradictory than a Christmas song written by a Jewish composer? Consider that among the many Christmas songs written by Jewish composers are "White Christmas," "I'll Be Home for Christmas," "The Christmas Song" ("Chestnuts Roasting on an Open Fire"), and "Santa Baby." Indeed, many Jewish people embrace the spirit of the holiday and enjoy singing these and other songs. Why not? There is a way to enjoy the Christmas season even if one doesn't believe Jesus was the Messiah.[4]

Perhaps more surprisingly, Richard Dawkins says, "I actually love most of the genuine Christmas carols,"[5] and the atheist R. Elisabeth Cornwell sings songs like "Silent Night."[6] Why not? Why should Christians have that experience all to themselves? There is something soaring and beautiful about many Christmas songs, and it can be an uplifting experience to sing them, especially in a group. Just as a horror movie fan may relish the experience of fright even though she doesn't believe that the monsters on the screen are real, so too one can enjoy the experience of transcendence in singing Christmas songs even though one doesn't believe the stories they tell are true. In fact, it would be a mistake to try to change the lyrics and keep the tune. The original lyrics allow us to enter another world for a moment, much as we do when we watch a movie. It is an experience not to be missed. Given this experience of Christmas songs, some atheists are willing to play along and ask the question, What else can we find of value in religion that we can appropriate for other purposes? As mentioned, one leading candidate is meditation.

There is a difference between prayer and meditation, but there is no clear line between them. There can be meditative elements of prayer, especially when prayer is scripted rather than spontaneous. In such cases, the act of prayer may put a person in a particular state of mind like that reached in meditation. Likewise, meditation is often rooted in religion and may have a prayerful quality to it or may include some kind of religious reflection.

Despite the connections, the practice of meditation likely predates organized religion. James Kingsland, the author of *Siddhartha's Brain*, speculates that it was probably discovered countless times by people staring at fire or perhaps water. The relaxed state of mind one enters in meditation can be thought of as the opposite of the fight-or-flight response.[7] It is thus a welcome antidote to anxiety and edginess. This is not the place to explore the science of meditation, but suffice it to say, it works. MRI and fMRI studies show visible changes in the brains of meditators.[8]

Nearly everyone would like to deal better with stress, and meditation can be very helpful in that regard. The practice of meditation is not just about entering a calm, relaxed, and focused state of mind while sitting cross-legged on a mat for twenty minutes a day. It is about slowing reaction time. Live broadcasts of award shows typically have a seven-second delay so that they can mute obscenities. Meditation does not produce a seven-second delay—that would be way too much—but in my experience meditation does delay reaction time to upsetting stimuli by a fraction of a second, allowing me to reconsider my response. I do and say fewer regrettable things today, as a result of meditation, than I did when I started meditating fifteen years ago. Progress is almost imperceptibly slow over any short period of time but undeniable over any long period of time, like watching grass grow.

Sam Harris has unapologetically spent a great deal of time meditating with Hindus and Buddhists, and he has even written a book about it, *Waking Up*.[9] There is nothing necessarily religious about meditation. As mentioned, its origins probably predate any religious connection. But for better or worse, the practice of meditation has been preserved within religious contexts. So, in learning the practice and theory of meditation, one can't avoid looking to and learning from religious people. In particular, Hindus and Buddhists have much to offer. Some Buddhists, of course, are atheists, so this may make the learning process more palatable for atheists. And there is a growing shelf of books aimed at teaching and explaining meditation to secular readers.

Eastern religions are generally bound up with Eastern philosophies—Buddhism, for example, is both a religion and a philosophy. In addition to meditation, there is much else that an atheist can gather and learn from Buddhism. Tibetan Buddhism even offers a prayer for the "four immeasurables"—loving kindness, compassion, sympathetic joy, and equanimity—that atheists may find appealing:

> May all beings have happiness and the cause of happiness.
> May they be free of suffering and the cause of suffering.
> May they never be disassociated from the supreme happiness which is without suffering.
> May they remain in the boundless equanimity, free from both attachment to close ones and rejection of others.

Notice that no deity is invoked or petitioned. The prayer takes the form of a wish that all beings will be well. The intention is to promote the development of loving kindness, compassion, sympathetic joy, and equanimity in oneself by wishing the same for all beings.

Western atheists may be more comfortable looking to and learning from an Eastern religion that is also a philosophy and one that was not the religion of their upbringing. But that should not stop anyone from mining Western religions for gems. Prayer, much more than meditation, is an essential part of Judaism, Christianity, and Islam. There is much that an atheist will find distasteful about prayer in which one prostrates oneself before an unseen God who demands worship in exchange for sometimes supposedly granting favors. Of course, no religious believer would accept that unkind description of prayer, but with some justification that is how it looks to many atheists. When an atheist looks at prayer that way, however, she sees only the surface. She does not see the interior benefits. To condemn prayer on these terms is akin to condemning meditation as a waste of time during which one sits silently in an uncomfortable position. That is a fair assessment at first glance, but further examination reveals much more. You do not need to subscribe to any particular religion or believe in any God at all to meditate. The same is true of prayer. It is possible to be a praying atheist, a "pray-theist" if you like.

People who do not belong to any particular religion can pray, and even atheists have been known to throw a Hail Mary pass or utter a plea of desperation in a foxhole. But that's not what we're concerned with here. Prayer has been described as speaking to God. But we do not need to think that someone is listening to speak to them—we do not even have to think that they exist. Lots of people talk to their deceased spouses. Many of them may think that their spouses can still somehow hear them in the afterlife. But other people just find it helpful to talk to their deceased spouses even though they don't think the spouses hear them. What could be the value in speaking to someone who cannot hear you because they do not exist?

Consider the value of writing a letter to a deceased parent. The parent certainly will not read it, but writing the letter may be beneficial to the writer as a way of clarifying and expressing emotions such as loss, regret, anger, or forgiveness. For that matter, the letter does not have to be addressed to a deceased person. I have found it cathartic to write angry e-mails and never send them or show them to anyone. So let's not be so quick to dismiss prayer just because we don't think anyone is listening. If the atheist is right, people have been praying for millennia and no one has been listening, but perhaps it still does some good.

Let's consider what the value and benefits of prayer might be once the religious baggage is stripped away. One clear benefit is expression. We have feelings, thoughts, and emotions in need of expression. Some people may express themselves in discussion with friends and family, others in making music or listening to music. For some, writing in a journal does the trick. Prayer, though, can have a performative dimension that makes it effective and appropriate for expressing certain thoughts and feelings. In that sense, prayer for the atheist can be like singing in the car or singing in the shower. No one is listening, and that is just fine.

For the atheist, such as myself, proper humility is a difficult virtue to cultivate. Without a God, it's easy to lose proper perspective and a sense of our small place in the world. Worse, lack of humility may become arrogance, a particularly off-putting personality trait. Lack of humility is also connected to an inflated sense of control. And this sense of control sets us up for disappointment to which we may react with anger and frustration.

The words an atheist chooses in prayer are optional, and they can be spoken silently or out loud—whatever works best for the individual.[10] As with the Tibetan Buddhist prayer for the four immeasurables, no one needs to be addressed. If you have difficulty in praying without addressing someone or something directly, then there are some options. The words can be addressed to "God" in scare quotes, or to the universe, or to nature. St. Paul describes a Greek altar dedicated to the "unknown god." The Greeks were apparently covering their bases with whatever god or gods they had missed or dismissed.

For the atheist, it can make sense to address "the nonexistent god" in prayer. God is thus conceived as a kind of invisible friend, but there is no delusion as to his actual existence. It is just a matter of making sense of a dialogue without a partner.[11]

My experience is that humility and gratitude are linked; I gain humility by expressing gratitude. Without God, the nonbeliever might not know to whom gratitude should be expressed.[12] Of course there are people in our lives to whom and for whom we are grateful, both for their presence and for the things they do and give. But the believer may have an easier time thanking God for other things like health, safety, and life itself. The atheist, though, can still find a way to express gratitude in the abstract. For my part, I find it helpful to write a daily list of things and people I am grateful for. For some atheists this may suffice, but, in addition, I find it helpful to express in prayer my gratitude for health, safety, family, and life itself. This is simply to recognize my good fortune.

The atheist Richard Dawkins notes that "We are going to die, and that makes us the lucky ones. Most people are never going to die because they are never going to be born. The potential people who could have been here in my place but who will in fact never see the light of day outnumber the sand grains of Arabia."[13] I don't suppose that Dawkins prays to express gratitude for the good fortune of having been born, but I do. Cognitively calculating my good fortune is not enough; for me, it requires affective expression. Again, the gratitude can be expressed to "God," the universe, or to no one in particular. It can be like putting a message in a bottle and throwing it in the ocean without expecting anyone to ever read it. So, instead of seeing such prayer as an unfortunate relic from a religious past, one can see it as a ritual in which one pauses to get proper perspective.

There is value in rituals to the extent that they remind us of who we are. Consider the value of saying hello or shaking hands. The ritual does not offer deep connection with the other person, but it is a way of pausing and recognizing the other person and their relation to us. Ritual can be a matter of acting "as if." For example, when we play hide-and-seek with a small child we act as if we have difficulty finding them. The child knows, and we know, that this is a farce. So why do we do it? Because there is something to be gained in enacting the ritual.[14] Likewise, prayer can be a valuable ritual for an atheist. It is not a matter of the kind of deceptive fictionalism that we discussed in chapter 4. Rather, it is a way of deriving benefits by acting "as if." In order to derive benefits, one does not need to believe or even pretend to believe.

Prayer as expression of humility and gratitude may sound all right, but for many people, prayer is essentially sacrifice and petition. Prayer is *do ut des*—I give so that you will give. I humble myself by getting on my knees and praising you, and in turn you give me what I ask for. Implicit in this contract is the threat that if God doesn't come through, then neither will I next time. This is probably the most primitive form of prayer.

For the prescientific human being, the world appeared to be governed by divine whim and will. The lesson of reciprocity learned from human interaction would have been transposed onto divine interaction. Trade and reciprocity work clearly and easily enough between humans who each have something that the other wants. But what could a God want that a human has? Food and drink must have seemed like logical answers, and so animal sacrifices were common in primitive religions and are even called for in the Old Testament. But the God of the Old Testament wanted something more: exclusivity.

He promised to have a special relationship with the Hebrew people if they would worship only him.

One of the problems with this kind of contractual relationship with God is that he seems to break his end of the bargain all the time. But that couldn't be—it couldn't be God's fault. And so people look for what they did wrong. Was it the wrong kind of animal sacrifice? Was it done in the wrong way? Was there not enough? Were we not faithful enough in honoring our contract of exclusivity with God? It's clear how all these worries lead to the remedy of ritual to ensure that things will be done right on our end. This kind of prayer and sacrifice is motivated by anxious fear, not sincere love. But, as with superstition, people cling to it despite its ineffectiveness.

Studies show that prayer does nothing to heal the sick; patients who are prayed for do no better than those who are not prayed for.[15] Of course, believers will respond that God refuses to be tested in such ways. Believers will say that God answers all prayers. It's just that sometimes the answer is no, or not yet, or "I love you too much to give you that." God works in mysterious and unseen ways. Only he knows why he grants some petitions and not others. The very nature of this response makes it impossible to falsify or disprove. It may be correct, but it offers no reason for the nonbeliever to take it seriously. Actually, when you think about it, petitioning God in prayer makes no sense if he is conceived as all-good, all-loving, and all-powerful. Why would an all-knowing God need to be coaxed into doing something good for someone he loves? Petitioning God in prayer only makes sense if we think of him as a powerful but imperfect being who doesn't know everything and either needs to be flattered or needs to be told about what we think we need or want. An all-good, all-loving, and all-powerful God wouldn't require petitionary prayer for his own sake, but only for the sake of the person. We need to ask, but God doesn't really need to be asked.

Petitionary prayer can benefit a person as an expression of longing, hope, or desire. Much as singing a song about one's hopes or desires does nothing directly to bring them about but can still be valuable as an expression of hopes and desires, so too with prayer. Prayer in this sense is a kind of poetry of the heart. And as such it is something that atheists need not deny themselves. An atheist can express a wish or articulate a plan in prayer as a way of envisioning a positive outcome and thereby increasing its likelihood through suitable actions. As songs can inspire us, so too can prayers.

Prayer doesn't change the world for the person, but prayer can change the person for the world. As a result of prayer, the person sees the world differently and is better able to act to change the world. Much of this is a matter of positive thinking, autosuggestion, and the placebo effect. In praying, one has done something that one thinks will have a positive effect, much like taking a placebo (a sugar pill that one thinks is medicine). In the case of the believer, it can take the form of believing that God has a purpose and a plan in mind; this can make difficulties seem like temporary setbacks rather than permanent failures. For the atheist, prayer can deliver proper perspective on one's small place in the cosmos and gratitude for one's good fortune. Such perspective casts things in a positive light and can foster productive action. In *The 7 Laws of Magical Thinking*, Matthew Hutson says, "Counter to the saying about horseshoes working even if you don't believe in them, it turns out they work *because* you believe in them."[16] In other words, not believing but still using a horseshoe is nonetheless a way of believing, and an effective way at that. The same can be true of petitionary prayer for the atheist. For example, expressing a desire for a job in prayer can be a way of setting up a positive expectation and self-fulfilling prophecy.[17] As Hutson says, "If you picture yourself getting a particular job, you'll walk into the interview with confidence and make a strong impression on the employer, which might get you that job."[18] This is not magic, and there is no "secret."

Prayer may be best when it is spontaneous and personal, like singing in the car or shower. But just as it is difficult to make up new songs every day, so too with new prayers. Most standard prayers have heavy religious baggage—it would be surprising if they didn't. Consider the Lord's Prayer, also known as the Our Father. It expresses some nice thoughts on forgiveness, but aside from that, it is a distinctly Christian prayer—it does not fit with the theologies of Judaism or Islam, for example. There are some prayers, though, that despite their religious origin, express wisdom that is nondenominational and even nonreligious. In concluding this chapter, let's look at two such prayers, both dear to recovery groups.

Consider the Serenity Prayer: "God, grant me the serenity to accept the things I cannot change, courage to change the things I can, and wisdom to know the difference."

These words of Reinhold Niebuhr are a font of wisdom. God can be swapped for "God," Tao, logos, nature, current of the universe, whatever. Serenity is peace of mind, as discussed in chapter 2. Etymologically, to be "serene" is to be clear, like a sky without clouds. We want a mind clear of worries and disruption despite what may be going on around us. Ironically, the prayer asks for the serenity to do the things necessary to achieve serenity. So which came first, the chicken or the egg, the serenity or the actions? Eggs aside, the serenity helps us to take the actions, and the actions help us to achieve serenity. We do not have complete serenity at first, nor do we practice the actions perfectly at first, but in time a degree of serenity is achieved that makes the actions easier. And as the actions become easier the serenity is more easily and more perfectly maintained.

So what about the actions? The first action is a kind of nonaction. Some things, like dead pets and annoying coworkers, we cannot change. The choice is ours, then, whether to try to change them anyway or try to find a way to be at peace with them. This leads us to the action of trying to change the things we can. Serenity is sought for the acceptance, and courage is sought for the action of change. But in truth, courage is also required for acceptance, and serenity is also required for the action of change. What we can definitely change is ourselves. I cannot change my coworker, but I can change my attitude toward him, to one of acceptance and compassion rather than resentment and ill will. With practice we can come to control our own emotional state and acceptance, but we never have that kind of control over another person. As the Stoics taught, we can at best *influence* another person or a situation. And such an attempt at influence inevitably comes at a price in terms of time, energy, or money. Perhaps the price spent will turn out to have been a good investment that pays dividends, or perhaps it will not.

Acceptance requires courage in the form of trusting the wisdom of nonaction. Similarly, the action of change requires serenity, the calm required in initiating and following through on action. Importantly, the prayer concludes with a petition for wisdom. Wisdom is acquired through living and learning from one's successes and failures. It is relatively easy to be willing to accept what we cannot change and act to change what we can. With proper reflection, who would deny this is what they aim to do anyway? The difficult thing is to know the difference. Such insight does not come from books but from experiences. Still, we can learn well, or not at all, from our experiences. So, "'God,' make me a quick learner!" There are some things that I *can* change but that I *should not*. These by default are really things that I cannot change—I cannot change them if I want to keep my serenity intact. These are the things it takes time and experience to learn to discern. Quickly, by comparison, we can learn to stop trying to change and learn to start accepting that we cannot rouse a dead horse by beating it. Slowly, we learn the restraint to resist trying to get more out of a live horse than will be productive in the long run.

We don't really know if a change or other occurrence is good until we consider it in the long run.

Rather than react with strong emotions, I need to pause and say, "Maybe it's a good thing or maybe it's a bad thing. Only time will tell, and I will do my best to make a good thing of it."

"Give and you will receive." This is one message of the Prayer of St. Francis. We always have more than at least some other person, in fact probably more than many people. Giving our time, money, energy, attention, or whatever we may have to someone who has less makes us appreciate what we have and feel "rich." The good feelings that result not just from the comparison—but from the gratitude and the empowerment—make us magnets for good to come in return. No magic is involved, but the positive feelings giving birth to and being born from positive thoughts lead to positive words and actions, which attract like in kind. Again, no magic, no secret. People just like to do things for and with positive people.

Consider the Prayer of St. Francis:

> Lord, make me an instrument of Thy peace;
> Where there is hatred, let me sow love;
> Where there is injury, pardon;
> Where there is error, the truth;
> Where there is doubt, the faith;
> Where there is despair, hope;

Where there is darkness, light;
And where there is sadness, joy.

O Divine Master,
Grant that I may not so much seek
To be consoled, as to console;
To be understood, as to understand;
To be loved as to love.

For it is in giving that we receive;
It is in pardoning that we are pardoned;
And it is in dying that we are born to eternal life. Amen.

Although religious in origin, the words demand little in theology. The references to Lord and Divine Master are nicely vague and can be swapped out for "God," Tao, nature, logos, current of the universe, whatever. This is a prayer for kindness and compassion, asking that I may be relieved of the bondage of self. It asks nothing for myself, though it recognizes that in directing myself toward others I ultimately benefit much more than I would in self-seeking. Maladies of turmoil, hatred, injury, doubt, despair, darkness, and sadness afflict human life. The prayer does not ask that I be spared of these. It asks instead that I help spare others by bringing to them the gifts of peace, love, pardon, faith, hope, light, and joy. Ironically, though, it will be in bringing these gifts to others that I will receive them myself. This is no mystery and requires no divine intervention. Teachers know that they learn by teaching their students; parents know the greatest love and reward is in loving their children.

Obsessive concern for ourselves, our own problems and situations, does more harm to us than does anything external. Focusing on others and helping them is the key to unlocking the chains that keep us in misery. To receive these gifts we must seek to do for others rather than to have things done for us. Though it may be our tendency to seek to be understood, loved, given to, and pardoned, we will receive these gifts most effectively in giving away what little we have in order to understand, love, give to, and pardon others. We make ourselves magnets and targets of the kindness and goodwill of others by being kind and of goodwill. Not that this is the prime motivation. How could it be, for, at first, who would believe it works? Desperation is the initial motivation, and the relief we feel in forgetting about ourselves for a short time is the initial reward that allows us to persist until the unexpected results come.

The closing line of the St. Francis prayer reveals how the psychology is consistent with Christian theology: only in dying do we come fully to life. But we do not need to accept the Christian theology to see and accept the profound wisdom of the psychology. In fact, aside from the closing line, the prayer could work just as well within an atheistic Buddhist context. The self and its desires are the source of all suffering. Getting outside the self, reaching out to another to relieve her suffering, unwittingly relieves my suffering.

8

A SKEPTIC'S GUIDE TO RELIGIONS, SPIRITUAL AND SECULAR

No one can define religion, but most people know it when they see it. That is because religion is a family resemblance term with no necessary or sufficient conditions.[1] This means that there is no single thing that all religions have in common that makes them religions. Belief in God is not necessary for a religion—some forms of Buddhism, for example, do not involve belief in a God or gods. A moral code is not sufficient, not enough to qualify something as a religion—there are secular humanist philosophies that endorse moral codes but which are not religions. Instead of necessary or sufficient conditions, religions share a network of overlapping characteristics. This is where we get the comparison to family resemblance.

For a group of people to share a family resemblance it is not necessary for them to share any single characteristic—like a prominent chin. Nor is it enough for any random person to have a particular characteristic—like a large nose—for that person to share the family resemblance. The random person may have a large nose like many members of the family and yet not be a member of the family and thus not share the family resemblance. The large nose is not sufficient. Still, it is not difficult to pick out typical examples of religions. As noted, not all religions recognize gods or a God, but recognizing gods or a God is one of the typical traits that count toward sharing the family resemblance of religion. And it is the most important trait under consideration in this book.

Experience of the divine is a trait typically associated with religion. St. Paul was blinded by bright light and fell from his horse on the road to Damascus. But how many people really have an experience of the divine that drives them to their knees? Most people are just told to get on their knees. Perhaps St. Paul had epilepsy and suffered from temporal lobe seizures or perhaps his experience was genuine. Or perhaps both. Anyone having such an experience today would be obliged to consult a doctor and examine her experience skeptically. Perhaps such a person could be excused for taking her experience to be genuine despite a medical explanation for its cause. In any event, most people do not have such profound experiences. They simply take on the religion of their parents, and they blame only themselves for lacking profound experience of God.

It is hard to fault parents for taking children to church and teaching them their faith. Such practice is well meaning, but it also deprives the child of genuine choice. Infant baptism makes a choice for the child that would be better left for the adult individual. Of course, parents make many choices for their children in terms of what they will eat, how they will dress, where they will go to school, and so on. Arguably, the parents' choice to baptize and religiously educate a child is an even more vital and important decision, one that should not be left for the child to make. Still, it would be beneficial if more religions made more of a place for individual decisions to accept or reject the religion at various stages of maturation. A second baptism of adults might take place at age twenty-one or twenty-five or thirty. Of course, people raised in a particular religion would be inclined to accept such a second baptism, but they could at least be encouraged to give it serious thought, to look at the foundations of the religion and to explore other possibilities.[2]

Without a mature adult choice of religion, too many people are left with hollow worship. Indeed, worship is a practice closely connected to religion, though it does not belong exclusively to religion. As David Foster Wallace put it in his Kenyon College commencement address, "In the day-to-day trenches of adult life, there is actually no such thing as atheism. There is no such thing as not worshiping. Everybody worships."[3] This is wrong on the face of it, but right in the insight it expresses. Wallace is referring to the tendency to be obsessed with money, power, material possessions, fame, beauty, and so on—false idols, a religious person might call them. But such obsession does not mean that one is not an atheist. A power-mad atheist is still an atheist. Wallace's statement is also wrong in characterizing such obsession as worship. Obsession does not necessarily constitute worship. In fact, it rarely does, not in the relevant religious sense of the term. Worship involves the feeling and expression of reverence and adoration. People in pursuit of power do not often revere or adore power; they revel in it or crave it. Power is something they want to possess; it is not something outside themselves that they place on a pedestal. The same is true for money, fame, beauty, and so on. It is possible to worship something other than a God, but Wallace's metaphorical extension of the term "worship" is relevantly different from the religious sense.

Wallace takes worship for granted and does not point out what an odd practice and phenomenon religious worship is. An all-powerful God wouldn't need worship because such a God wouldn't need anything, certainly not the praise and adoration of mere mortals. Of course, most gods in most times and places have *not* been conceived as all-powerful, and thus they did want human worship as testimony to their greatness. Such gods were like insecure kings who wanted people to bow down before them. Worship of that kind is distasteful, and an all-loving God wouldn't want it. An all-loving God would only want worship if it benefitted the person. In such a case, worship might be good for the person as a means of gaining perspective and humility.

Worship might also be just an outward sign or manifestation of recognizing the awesome power and benevolence of God. This may be akin to the experience of the sublime in nature where one feels in awe at a safe distance from a thunderstorm or tornado or feels overwhelmed by the immensity of the Grand Canyon. Beauty too may call forth a desire to worship, particularly the beauty of the human form. There may be a natural desire to seek such experiences whether in religion, nature, or art. But the desire does not seem universal. Wallace is wrong in his characterization of worship as inescapable. He does seem to be right, though, in cautioning against filling the God-shaped hole with something else.

People have a tendency to become obsessed with things in a manner that might aptly be described as religious. Religion fills a need for community, but there are other alternatives. A Cubs fan may go to the church of Wrigley Field "religiously"—that is, faithfully, that is, with dedicated commitment. Cubs fans may be a particularly good case in point, but what is true of Cubs fans is true of sports fans in general. They have an emotional devotion to a team and to certain players. Here we can see something close to worship in the religious sense, and perhaps rightly so. Nearly anyone who ever saw Michael Jordan play felt reverence and awe. Indeed, I say that as a Knicks fan. And what, after all, is the Hall of Fame at Cooperstown but a place to worship baseball idols?

From an evolutionary perspective, religion validated codes of reciprocity and joined people together with those of their tribe. One of its main functions was as a bonding mechanism, and this remains true today in the secular world of sports fandom. We bond with those who root for the same team. Sports fandom, in this way, plays a useful role in providing an outlet for the need to bond over shared admiration and commitment.

Of course, not everyone is a sports fan, and, alas, many of the alternatives are not as benign. Take nationalism for example. The tendency to bond against a common enemy is as old as the species and is imprinted in our DNA. We see it play out in sports fandom when rivals like the Yankees and the Red Sox play. Hatred for the rival can be even stronger than love for one's team; it can be more intense anyway. The threats and acts of terrorists tend to catalyze nationalism at least for short periods of time, as we see excessive displays of national pride and excessive fears of the enemy.[4] Many people, of course, claim that God is on their side, but even an atheist can be susceptible to nationalism.

In an attempt to rationally rein in nationalism, a person may turn to politics. Cooler heads need to prevail, and demonizing the national enemy won't work. So far, so good. The problem comes when politics becomes "religious," when political ideology becomes unquestionable dogma, and when political leaders become secular saints. With smug superiority it is easy to think one sees the way and the solution that the jingoistic masses do not. Compromise becomes difficult when ideological rigidity sets in. The misplaced, religious longing for a savior and for salvation is nowhere as clear as in the political realm. The truth is that no one can save you but yourself. Others can help. Others may even be necessary, but they will never be sufficient. For that reason, it is wise to be wary of anyone who offers himself as a savior. Martyrs are bad, but saviors are worse. Martyrs can be genuine, although the false variety who require or anticipate praise and admiration are too common. Saviors who offer themselves as such or allow themselves to be cast in that role are pernicious. In the small groups of about one hundred that early humans lived in, it may have been true that a single person could know what was best for the group and take actions to achieve it. In large groups, however, no political saviors of that sort are possible. Our interests and concerns are too many and varied. Solutions and answers are to be found at the level of small groups and individuals. When large groups begin looking to a political savior, madness lies that way.

The French philosopher and sociologist Raymond Aron famously called Marxism the "opium of the intellectuals," and many have noted the religious quality of environmentalism.[5] Humanity may be headed toward a post-religious future, but most atheists are not there yet. Some atheists will scoff at this, but before they do they should ask themselves what "sacred games" they have invented to fill the religious vacuum.

Historically, religion has been unparalleled in its ability to provide comfort. Life is tough. In fact, it is often absurd. Comfort can be a byproduct of community; our burden is lessened in sharing it with others. Others may listen, console, and share their experience, strength, and hope. But some people seek more comfort than human fellowship can provide. In describing religion as the opiate of the masses, Karl Marx also called religion the "heart of a heartless world."[6] Marx was not condemning individuals for taking false comfort in religion. Rather, Marx understood why such comfort was sought and provided. Marx sought to change the world so that such comfort would no longer be needed or sought, but he did not succeed. A smaller percentage of people today may seek comfort in religion than did in Marx's day, but the need has not gone away. In fact, the world is just as absurd and people need comfort all the more.

Rejecting religion but seeking metaphysical comfort, some people like to describe themselves as "spiritual but not religious." They reject the dogma of organized religions but may have some nebulous conception of a higher power and perhaps a belief in fate. With its obvious root, "spirit," something nonmaterial, "spirituality" perpetuates belief in the supernatural. For those who reject supernatural belief, I suggest the description "philosophical but not religious" and the concept of "transcendence." Transcendence, as I conceive of it, is spirituality without the spirit, without the nonmaterial, without the supernatural. "Transcendence" fits perfectly well with the implications of phrases like "team spirit" or "national spirit" or "spirit of the age." With the connotations of moving beyond oneself and above the mundane, transcendence means connecting with others and feeling part of something greater than ourselves.

What so many people seek, even what some seek in spirits of the alcoholic variety, is transcendence. We want to move beyond the mundane circumstances and concerns of daily life to be a part of something greater, like a team, nation, or age—or church. Transcendence is difficult, even elusive, and so a ready-made ritual or religion is attractive, providing something tested and tangible for what is uncertain and intangible, the feeling of transcendence.

Playing on a team or singing in a choir can deliver the experience of transcendence for some people. One important trait or function of religion is providing transcendence in the form of fellowship. Fellowship is a matter of interacting with people who are simpatico, who get us, and who provide a place where we fit and belong. Many parts of society are competitive, the realm of work in particular. We compete not only with other producers or providers of the same goods and services, but also with our coworkers—with those who are supposed to be on our side. There can be comradery and fellowship at work, but too often there is strife.

A church can provide respite from the world of competition, a place where cooperation is prized over competition, a sanctuary in which we can be vulnerable, where we can help and be helped. But the number of people who experience that kind of fellowship at their church is far smaller than the number of people who would benefit from it. Some churches are too big and others too small; some seek to cultivate fellowship, and others don't. Clearly, churches and religious organizations do not have a monopoly on facilitating fellowship. Civic organizations, clubs, and informal groups of friends may often do a better job. But churches have an advantage in that, at least theoretically, people can come together as equals at church and can be vulnerable, humble, and helpful.[7] Secular substitutes are certainly possible, but they must be built rather than found ready-made.

Because secular substitutes for the fellowship found in churches are scarce, there are atheists in the choir.[8] There are also atheists in the pulpit, people who have lost their faith but don't feel confident moving on to a new profession.[9] Whereas the choir members' indulgence may be harmless, the preachers' pretending is not. For many people, identity is bound up with religion. In some ways, matters are easier when religion is also bound up with ethnicity. It is no contradiction to call oneself a Jewish atheist. Indeed, many Jewish atheists attend synagogue. The connections they feel with others who share their cultural heritage are enough to make them tolerate the talk of God. Likewise, though less common, there are Hindu atheists, like the Nobel Prize–winning economist Amartya Sen. Indeed, there are many Christian atheists who sing in choirs and sit in pews. This can cause cognitive dissonance, but it need not necessarily for those who are clear about their motives, whether those motives are to achieve transcendence by singing in the choir, or to enjoy the fellowship of a community, or to provide a moral structure for raising children. Personally, I think there are better secular alternatives available for these purposes, but such choices are individual and family matters.

I consider myself to be culturally Catholic, not in the sense of endorsing the teachings of the Church or belonging to a congregation, but simply in recognizing the tremendous influence of my Catholic upbringing and in identifying with others who share that framework. Much as an alcoholic will always be an alcoholic, I will always be a Catholic. You can call me a lapsed Catholic, a cultural Catholic, or an atheistic Catholic. I am a Catholic nonetheless. There is no God, but if there were, he would require that you abstain from meat on Fridays during Lent. I was not abused by priests—unless you count the one who put the fear of hell in me. In fact, a priest saved my life, and several priests encouraged me to think critically and independently such that I lost my faith.

9

CONFESSIONS OF A
RECOVERING CATHOLIC

In the Catholicism of my childhood, the point was to avoid hell. Heaven was too lofty a goal—purgatory was a reasonable aspiration. Hell was where you were going unless you got your act together—and no one really had their act together. We were all sinners in the hands of an angry God who loved us more than we could possibly understand. Purgatory was a saving grace for Catholics. I don't know how Protestants do without it. The Protestant claim to be saved because of faith and acceptance of Jesus Christ as lord and savior always struck me as facile. As a good Catholic I had that faith and that acceptance, but I was going to hell anyway if I missed mass on Sunday. That's what the pastor, the priest in charge of our parish, told us. Missing mass was a mortal sin, and if you died with a mortal sin on your soul you would go to hell. Because it was always a genuine possibility that a child would die in his sleep, missing mass was particularly dangerous. I had a plaque with that child's prayer: "Now I lay me down to sleep. I pray the Lord my soul to keep. But if I die before I wake, I pray the Lord my soul to take." Maybe I was just sensitive, but I found that prayer terribly disturbing.

If you missed mass, the only thing that would repair the damage was going to confession, receiving the sacrament of reconciliation. A personal, prayerful apology to God was not enough; it would not remove the mortal sin from your soul. If you missed mass on Sunday and survived the night and prayerfully apologized to God, but on your way to make confession and receive reconciliation on Monday you got run over by a truck and died, you were out of luck. You were going to hell.

For that matter, pretty much everyone else who was not baptized in the Catholic Church was going to hell too. Maybe some particularly good people who lived in other cultures and hadn't heard about Jesus could make it onto the wait list of purgatory and then eventually get into heaven. But Protestants and Jews were almost certainly going to hell because they knew about Jesus and the Catholic Church and yet they defiantly went their own way. Unbaptized babies were a more sympathetic case. They had done nothing wrong and had not rejected the church. However, if they died unbaptized and without coming into the church they could not enter heaven. For them, there was a special place called limbo. There was nothing bad about limbo; there was no pain and suffering there. But it was not heaven. Some adults who had not known of Jesus might be there too. This was the 1970s and 80s, and talk of limbo had faded in most places after the Second Vatican Council (1962–65). News of Vatican II had not reached my parish by then, though, or more truly some of its spirit had simply been ignored. I suspect this parish was a bit extreme for its time and place, but I don't think it was unique. I think the pastor was sincere. He really was concerned about the souls of his flock. He wanted to get them into heaven, or at least keep them out of hell. And there were plenty of things we could all do to help make that happen. There was no Calvinist sense of predestination.

The parish was not wealthy, and money weighed on the mind of the pastor. But not for a moment do I think that money motivated his talk of hell or his threat that missing mass was a mortal sin that would get you there. Nonetheless his talk was abusive. The pastor and the nuns, who reinforced that message at the Catholic grade school I attended in the parish, were sincere and well meaning but abusive nonetheless. Much as we can look at a parent who spanks a child as sincere and well meaning, yet abusive, so do I look at this priest and these nuns.

They taught that God was a mind reader. He knew what you were going to do before you did it, and yet everything you did was of your own free will. God could and should be prayed to. Poor children were starving in Cambodia and Africa, but if you prayed hard enough and sincerely enough, God might help them out. He never did, though. I guess that was our fault. The result was guilt. If one feeling marked my Catholic childhood, it was guilt. I was always doing, or if not doing, then thinking, something wrong. The ideal was to be unselfish in order to get into heaven, but if you were being unselfish in order to get into heaven, then wasn't that being selfish after all? Or at least self-interested? No one seemed to have answers to questions like these. Life was to be enjoyed but not too much. I was a serious child; I took things very seriously and literally.

Jesus didn't seem very nice, not very warm, not approachable. In the Gospel, he welcomed the children, but I didn't feel very welcome. He wasn't the soft and avuncular man I would have liked him to be. He wasn't like my Uncle Peter, or St. Francis, or the father from the *Brady Bunch*. Jesus had died for me and for my sins, not just the original sin of Adam and Eve but the sins that I would later commit in my life. It was the ultimate act of love that Jesus would die for us, but it was pretty hard to feel grateful for it.

At a certain point in grade school, the Garden of Eden was a myth, I think. In any event, not everything in the Bible was meant to be taken as literally true. Methuselah did not live to be 969 years old; that was just a way of saying that he lived to be very old. Thankfully,

I was never told that the earth was only 6,000 years old. That seems like a Protestant thing. There was more to history than was in the Bible—that seemed to be the message anyway.

One thing that was confusing was whether good behavior would be rewarded in this life or only in the next life. There were no clear answers. It appeared that God did sometimes reward people in this life, but that you couldn't expect him to. It was God's prerogative. So you could pray for certain good things, like catching a fish, or getting a hit, or having a girl like you. But it was up to God whether he would grant your request. It would be granted if it was God's will. That made prayer seem futile. If God's will was set, then what was the point of praying? I guess that without the prayer, God definitely wasn't going to come through.

All in all, I felt lucky and felt like God must like and favor me, but maybe not as much as other kids. I had never been popular with girls, and that kind of popularity is what I wanted most in life. God didn't seem to be answering any prayers there. Or if he was answering them, he was saying no. That was the odd thing about prayer—it was a matter of convincing an all-loving, all-knowing, all-powerful God that you knew better than he did what was good for you or that even if you didn't, God should give it to you anyway. God could be bargained with. You could promise to be good in certain ways (I won't fight with my sister) or you could promise to do certain things (I'll give money to the poor). You could even run an end around by praying to a saint for intercession. St. Mary, the blessed virgin mother, was particularly powerful in that regard. She would listen and hear your prayer, and she could talk to her son on your behalf. She could soften him up and get him to do what you wanted. Of course, she wasn't guaranteed to do that, but she seemed to like getting the attention, and, as a woman, she was more approachable and sympathetic. She could work miracles, and she had appeared to children throughout the centuries, most famously at Lourdes. The age of miracles was still upon us. Indeed, in order to be canonized as a saint there had to be miracles to your name and credit. The miracles in the Bible, especially the New Testament, were to be taken literally. Some of the Old Testament might be a bit hazy and exaggerated from a storytelling perspective, but the New Testament was completely reliable. The Gospels were written by the apostles Matthew, Mark, Luke, and John. They were eyewitnesses, and they were inspired by the Holy Spirit in writing down the stories, or so I was taught.

In eighth grade, life wasn't going ideally well for me. It could have been much worse, of course, but it wasn't unfolding the way it would if my prayers could write the story. My parents were both deeply unhappy with life in general and with each other. I didn't amount to much as an athlete—not only would pro sports not be in my future, but neither would high school sports. My friends were fickle, sometimes glad to see me and counting me in, sometimes not. No girls really liked me, and this was hardest of all—I had the sense that if a pretty, nice girl liked me then nothing much else would matter. I could deal with and put up with a lot if the right girl really loved and cared for me.

One big thing did go my way, though: I got a full academic scholarship to the high school that I really wanted to attend. This had resulted from a divine bargain. I had prayed the rosary to Mary every Sunday as a petition, and I had promised to say the rosary every Sunday as thanks and an offering if accepted. For a while I made good on my end of the bargain, but sometime during my first year of high school I ceased to pray the rosary. I was already in the school and succeeding academically. I didn't foresee Mary or Jesus taking back what had been given to me, and besides, saying the rosary on Sunday afternoons was boring, time-consuming, and depressing: "pray for us sinners, now and at the hour of our death."

From the time I was very young, I had questions and concerns about what happened after death. Was there really a soul that lived on? What if death was the end? I had lots of questions, though I didn't ask them in grade school. I didn't sense that most kids took religion as seriously as I did, even those who were more dedicated to the church. I envied them. They seemed to have the proper balance of fulfilling obligations in the right spirit, and yet not being weighed down by guilt and confusion.

In high school, my freshman theology class was taught by an ancient Jesuit with a fun-loving streak. In general, I liked the Jesuits. They were smart, confident, capable, and worldly—a welcome change from the parish priest. The theme of the freshman theology course was something like "things in the Bible that aren't exactly so." I recall learning terms like "literary genre" and *Sitz im Leben*. There was a greater openness than I had encountered before. Protestants weren't all going to hell. In fact, I was given the assignment to visit a Sunday Protestant service. I don't think I was too impressed by what the Protestants had to offer, but I was impressed that a Jesuit priest would require us to attend such a service.

Freshman biology taught me the most important idea I've ever encountered, maybe the greatest idea and scientific discovery of all time, the theory of evolution. It has been called the universal acid, and for me it was—it dissolved everything it touched. More positively, it made sense of the world. There could be no immaterial soul in a world formed through a process of evolution. It did not make sense to think that God had simply injected a soul into the creature once it had become human. Without God there was no objective right and wrong—no divine command. There was only reciprocal altruism and the evolved inclination to treat kin well for the sake of disseminating genes. Even beauty disappeared—understood now as an appreciation for signals of health and other things that favored survival. In a flash, the theory of evolution had unweaved the rainbow and clipped the angel's wings.

Of course, many people accept the theory of evolution and still retain their Christian faith. It's difficult to do, though. It was much easier to be a Christian before Darwin, when one could believe that the biological world evinced the design of a creator rather than the spontaneous order of a blind process. Yes, God could be behind the process of evolution, having initiated it, perhaps even guiding it, but that was a big pill to swallow. It would have made much more sense for an all-loving, all-powerful God to have made the world all at once (or in seven days). The process of evolution is slow, painful, and imperfect—red in tooth and claw. Just think of all the needless suffering that God could have spared his creatures if he had made them all at once rather than through natural selection and survival of the fittest.

Even before the time of Darwin, and all the more so after him, the Bible had become an object of serious scholarly scrutiny. And the fruits of this scrutiny were served up in my sophomore theology course, which focused on biblical exegesis. Aided by *The Jerome Biblical Commentary* we examined scriptural passages with an eye to discovering who wrote them and why. Yes, the Bible was divinely inspired, but it was humanly authored. The Bible was not a single book, but a collection of books. And some books had multiple authors and editors. We learned about the Yahwist, Elohist, Priestly, and Deuteronomist authors who wrote the first five books of the Bible, and we learned about the source material they used. When

The Epic of Gilgamesh was rediscovered in 1853, the initial reaction was that its story of a flood provided confirmation of the biblical story of Noah. Only later did scholars come to realize that *Gilgamesh* is an earlier and independent flood story. It is a common literary form, the destruction of the world by fire or flood. Indeed, the Old Testament was full of stories and literary devices that it borrowed from older sources. The more one looked, the less history one found. There was little reason to think of Abraham and the patriarchs as historical figures. Worse, there was no evidence of Moses as a historical figure. There is no historical or archaeological evidence of Hebrews being enslaved in Egypt, and the story of the exodus appears to be the legendary story of the founding of a people akin to the *Aeneid*. The verifiable historical record begins quite late, perhaps with the House of David, though even there the details in the biblical accounts cannot be accepted as strictly historical.

The haziness of the Old Testament would have been all right, if the New Testament were unassailable. Unfortunately, though, it too became incredible in light of scholarly scrutiny. Like most Christians, I had conflated the stories of the four Gospels to make a single unified narrative. Our sophomore teacher was not a priest, but he was a devout Catholic. His philosophy and pedagogy, though, was that a belief unchallenged was not worth having. He had a Yale divinity degree and he shared it with us. The Gospels, we learned, were not only written by four different authors; they were written for four different audiences and contained inconsistent details and some outright contradictions. Worse, the authors were not the apostles or disciples who gave their names to the Gospels. The Gospels were not eyewitness accounts—the apostles and original disciples were illiterate, Aramaic-speaking fishermen. The authors of the gospels, by contrast, were literate and wrote in Greek (not Aramaic).

The flight into Egypt is found in only one Gospel (Matthew 2:13–23) and is clearly meant to mimic and allude to the flight out of Egypt by Moses. Surely, if this were an historical event, all of Jesus's followers would have known about it and made it part of any retelling of the life story of Jesus. The story of the virgin birth is in only two Gospels (Matthew 1:18–25 and Luke 1:26–38). Again, that would be the kind of detail one would expect in any retelling, if true. Worse, stories of virgin birth were incredibly common in the ancient world as ways of signaling special or divine status. Mithras, for example, was said to have been born of a virgin. In light of all this, I asked my teacher if he believed that Jesus was born of a virgin. He said he did. I asked why. He said that he just did. The message was that faith could trump evidence and perhaps reason. I respected my teacher for his honest answer, and I certainly respected his impressive knowledge and erudition. But I lost a little respect for him because of his unwillingness to face the facts. I could not and would not walk right up to the edge of unbelief only to retreat. The cognitive dissonance was already ringing in my head. I couldn't take any more. Applying what I later came to understand was Ockham's razor, I preferred the simpler explanation: there was no God.

Junior year theology was disappointing, mostly because of a young and inexperienced teacher who tried too hard to be cool and repeatedly called me by the wrong name. I had heard of Nietzsche and Sartre by then, and I might even have read a little on my own. We did not read these philosophers for class, but we did read a summary piece about the atheism of Jean-Paul Sartre. I admired the bravery of a person who would declare that there is no God and no God-given meaning of life and who would face the world as it is and forge his own meaning. Of course, Sartre's forebear in this regard was Nietzsche, who had boldly proclaimed that God is dead. For someone who had cowered in fear of God and fear of hell and who had suspected that he was actually cowering in fear of a bogeyman, the models of Sartre and Nietzsche were inspirational. I took pleasure in reading and quoting them to the shocked dismay of friends and classmates.

None of this was entirely pleasant, however. The loss of God was far more traumatic than the loss of Santa Claus. Life could not just move on as if it were no big deal. This is why Nietzsche's madman, who delivers the news of the death of God, asks what we shall do now that we have unchained the earth from its sun. God was the center, the point around which my life orbited. Nietzsche's madman goes on to wonder, "What festivals of atonement, what sacred games shall we have to invent?" In other words, what will provide meaning for our lives?

I was angry. I felt like I had been lied to for most of my life. People who knew better or should have known better had misinformed me. Life would have been a lot happier if I had simply been told the truth from the start. Instead, I had premised my behavior and my plans on the idea that there was a God who was watching me and who demanded certain actions and attitudes. As Nietzsche depicts it, the loss of God sets us adrift on stormy seas—it is terrifying and exhilarating. Most people who have glimpsed the truth will retreat rather than accept the responsibility. But the truth is also exhilarating with the responsibility and opportunity that it makes available. On a smaller scale we experience such responsibility in starting our first job, or going away to college, or having sex for the first time, or becoming parents. This particular large-scale exhilaration, though, is available only to those who lose God, as opposed to those who never had God. Those who are raised as atheists will never know the terror and exhilaration that the believer feels at the loss of God. The only similar experience might be the death of a parent at a young age. For the young atheist this could be a similar loss of center. Of course for the young believer the loss of a parent is also awful, but the believer will at least have the consolation that God loves them and has a plan.

What made me most angry was the realization that there was no cosmic justice. Whereas I previously had believed that God would make all things right in the end, I now realized that would not happen. There was this life, and that was all. Happiness in this life was all that mattered, and I was not very happy.

It is a testimony to the intellectual honesty of the Jesuits who taught me in high school that I chose to continue my education at a Jesuit university. There were several reasons behind my choice, but my budding atheism did not preclude studying with the Jesuits. Far from it, I had a Jesuit education to thank for opening my eyes and for encouraging me to ask tough questions and demand good answers. I majored in philosophy and was disappointed with how much and how often Thomas Aquinas came up in my classes. But it was the right major for me. After college I did my graduate training in philosophy at a large public university. This was the first time in my education that I shared the classroom with a majority of non-Catholics. Of course, in some sense I had years ago ceased to be a Catholic myself, but I was still culturally Catholic. I always will be. For that reason, I had no hesitation in accepting a job offer to teach philosophy at a Catholic college. I deeply identify with my Catholic students.

Though very few students these days have had the fear of hell put into them the way I did as a boy, we share a common base of experience. Regrettably, most students have not been taught to question and interrogate their faith the way I was taught to by the Jesuits in high school. And so I hope to give them some of that experience. The Catholic tradition has always embraced philosophy, attempting to find a fit between faith and reason. This has not always been true in the Protestant tradition. Luther declared reason to be a whore, and a deep suspicion of reason has characterized some strains of Protestantism ever since. There is some justification for this suspicion. As my own experience testifies, questioning religious belief can lead to the loss of religious faith. If what is at stake is one's immortal soul, then perhaps the questioning is not worth the risk. Then again, perhaps a faith that will not subject itself to scrutiny is not worth having. I am thankful that the Jesuits who taught me were of this mindset.

My mission as a teacher is to show students how to think, not what to think. Philosophy, in that sense, is more about questions than answers, and God is the most intriguing question of all. I have no answers for my students—God is not an answer. We study the classic arguments for the existence of God and we note the problems with the arguments. Some students find that the arguments bolster their faith; some find the arguments silly—you can't prove God. We also study Nietzsche and Sartre. Some students find them shocking, blasphemous, and awful. Others don't have much of a reaction. Some may have the reaction that I had as a student—that these are brave and bold thinkers who are willing to cast out onto stormy seas. I see my role as a teacher as akin to that of a therapist. I am there to facilitate, to help students to think and to formulate their own answers. I stay neutral in presenting thoughts and in moderating discussions. I believe I've done well in supporting the mission of the college, prompting students to critically examine their faith rather than passively accept it.

Philosophy is the most valuable tool we have for thinking about life, but of course philosophy does not exist in isolation. The two most important things that an educated person should learn are the theory of evolutionary science and the practice of biblical criticism—who wrote the books of the Bible and why. Philosophy must be informed by other sources of knowledge, particularly science. Science can't answer philosophical questions, but it can and does supply information that is crucial in formulating educated answers to philosophical questions.

In the *Republic*, Plato describes a prisoner's escape from a cave where he had been chained by the neck and legs, watching shadows on the wall, taking that for the highest reality. The prisoner had been there all his life and had never experienced anything else. When he is mysteriously freed from the chains and ventures outside the cave, the prisoner is at first overwhelmed and takes a long time to adjust to the light of the sun and all that it reveals. As the story continues, the prisoner returns to the cave to tell others about what he has seen, but he meets with an unwelcome response. Life's journey can be even more complex than Plato's story. We sometimes escape from one cave only to find ourselves in another. This was my experience, escaping from the cave of dogmatic Catholicism only to take refuge in the cave of dogmatic atheism. Now, I realize that I do not know where the nesting caves end. I don't know what comes next. I may be at my destination. Or perhaps mysticism awaits me. All I know is that the question endures.

UPSHOT

"You're not an atheist. You're just an agnostic." That's what some readers will want to say to me. My response is that if what you mean by an atheist is someone who is certain that God does not exist, then you are right. But I don't think an atheist with doubts is the same thing as an agnostic. Rather, an agnostic claims to lack not only certainty but knowledge. By contrast, an atheist can claim to know there is no God without being certain of it, much as a believer can claim to know that there is a God without being certain of it. From the beginning, my point has been that no one can have 100 percent certain belief about anything. I have offered a sliding-scale epistemology in which belief can approach 100 percent certainty but never reach it. No bright line separates an agnostic from an atheist. Is a person who is 99 percent certain that there is no God an atheist? What about 90 percent? What about 60 percent? I would suggest that the best policy is to let people choose the label that makes most sense to them.

Choice is inevitable. Some people recoil at doubt because doubt seems paralyzing. But doubt is not the same thing as indecision. The religious believer makes the decision to continue practicing her faith in the midst of doubt to one degree or another. In his famous wager, the French philosopher and mystic Blaise Pascal advised people to bet on God, reasoning that you have everything to gain and nothing to lose. The atheist disagrees with Pascal and decides to live her life without belief in God, reasoning that there is actually much to lose in living a life devoted to a nonexistent God. Still, the atheist must admit to some doubt. There is at least some chance that she is wrong and that the potential loss is great. Doubt does not paralyze even the agnostic. In light of her lack of knowledge, the agnostic must choose how to live.

Though we must all decide how to live and where to place our bets, we cannot simply choose what to believe. Pascal famously counseled would-be believers to go to church and take the actions of believers in order to act their way into believing. His advice might work for a small range of people for whom belief in God is unsettled and yet is a live option. It would do nothing, however, to bring Richard Dawkins into the flock. Nor would the pope be moved to abandon belief in God by studying science more carefully and attending meetings of a secular humanist organization. What such efforts by Dawkins and the pope would do, though, is open their minds and soften their hearts by pushing them to recognize doubt and uncertainty.

The aim of this book has been to disrupt false certainty and to foster genuine uncertainty. Our inability to achieve certainty is not something to deny or be ashamed of. Instead it should be the source of intellectual humility and openness. It is important to be willing to change our minds even on the most important things, especially on the most important things. This does not mean that we should treat all claims and conclusions as equally valid, but that we should seek out the best arguments for views that we disagree with, especially concerning subjects where intelligent and educated people do in fact disagree with us. If we are right, we have nothing to fear from such exposure, and we may have something to learn. Our certainty may be diminished but our understanding of our own views will be improved. At the very least, we can learn to see those who disagree with us as not only fully human but capable of teaching us something.

NOTES

GENESIS: UNCERTAINLY YOURS

1. Kamel Daoud, *The Meursault Investigation*, trans. John Cullen (New York: Other Press, 2015), p. 139.

2. What I mean by "honest atheism" is akin to what Philip Kitcher calls "soft atheism" in *Life after Faith: The Case for Secular Humanism* (New Haven: Yale University Press, 2014). Kitcher says, "Soft atheism makes small concessions in the direction of agnosticism: while there is no basis for endorsing the transcendent, the bare possibility of some future justified acceptance cannot be eliminated" (pp. 23–24).

1. YOU CAN DOUBT ANYTHING, AND YOU SHOULD

Some material in this chapter was drawn from "A Reality Check to Form Your Philosophy," *Think* 15 (2015): 97–104.

1. Nick Bostrom, "Are You Living in a Computer Simulation?" *Philosophical Quarterly* 53 (2003), pp. 243–55; Nick Bostrom, "Why Make a Matrix? And Why You Might Be in One," in *More Matrix and Philosophy: Revolutions and Reloaded Decoded*, ed. William Irwin (Chicago: Open Court, 2005), pp. 81–92.

2. See Edmund L. Gettier, "Is Justified True Belief Knowledge?" *Analysis* 23 (1963), pp. 121–23. In this landmark article, Gettier showed that there are possible counterexamples to the traditional definition. The issue has been a subject of debate ever since. For our practical purposes, the scholarly debate need not concern us.

3. William James, *The Will to Believe* (New York: Dover Publications, 1956), p. 12.

4. William Irwin, "Authorial Declaration and Extreme Actual Intentionalism: Is Dumbledore Gay?" *Journal of Aesthetics and Art Criticism* 73 (2015), pp. 141–47.

5. See Nassim Nicholas Taleb, *The Black Swan: The Impact of the Highly Improbable* (New York: Random House, 2007).

6. Some philosophers would argue that the laws of logic and mathematics hold true in all possible worlds. I disagree.

7. Jack Huberman, *The Quotable Atheist* (New York: Nation Books, 2007), p. 306.

8. George Cotkin, *Existential America* (Baltimore: Johns Hopkins University Press, 2003), p. 17.

9. Alexis Chabot, "Cruel Atheism," *Sartre Studies International* 22 (2016), p. 59.

10. William James, *The Varieties of Religious Experience* (Lexington, KY: Renaissance Classics, 2012), p. 25.

2. LIVING WITH DOUBT

Some material in this chapter was drawn from "God Is a Question, Not an Answer," *The Stone* (blog), *New York Times*, March 27, 2016, SR8.

1. Miguel de Unamuno, *Tragic Sense of Life*, trans. J. E. Crawford Fitch (New York: Dover, 1954), p. 93.

2. As told by Rabbi Simeon Kolko in correspondence.

3. Mother Teresa, *Mother Teresa: Come Be My Light: The Private Writings of the Saint of Calcutta*, ed. Brian Kolodiejchuk (New York: Doubleday, 2007), pp. 187, 192–93.

4. John D. Caputo, *Hoping Against Hope: Confessions of a Postmodern Pilgrim* (Minneapolis: Fortress Press, 2015), p. 62.

5. Thomas Merton, *New Seeds of Contemplation* (New York: New Directions Books, 2007), p. 105.

6. Merton, pp. 12–13.

7. Richard Feynman, BBC *Horizon* interview, 1981, https://www.youtube.com/watch?v=I1tKEvN3DF0.

8. Denis Brian, *The Voice of Genius: Conversations with Nobel Scientists and Other Luminaries* (Cambridge, MA: Perseus, 1995), p. 49.

9. Damon Linker, "Why Doubt Is So Difficult," *The Week*, March 29, 2016, http://theweek.com/articles/615132/why-doubt-difficult.

10. Jesse Bering, *The Belief Instinct: The Psychology of Souls, Destiny, and the Meaning of Life* (New York: W.W. Norton, 2011), pp. 195–96.

11. Stephen Batchelor, *The Faith to Doubt: Glimpses of Buddhist Uncertainty* (Berkeley: Counterpoint, 2015), p. 15.

12. Herman Melville, *Moby Dick* (New York: Barnes & Noble, 2003), chapter 85, p. 436.

13. Epictetus, *Discourses*, Books 3-4. *The Encheiridion* (Loeb Classical Library No. 218), trans. W. A. Oldfather (Cambridge: Harvard University Press, 1928), section 8, p. 491.

14. Rainer Maria Rilke, *Letters to a Young Poet*, trans. M. D. Herter Norton (New York: W.W. Norton, 1962), p. 13.

3. WHAT DO YOU MEAN BY "GOD"?

1. John Hick, "A Philosophy of Religious Pluralism," in *A John Hick Reader*, ed. Paul Badham (Eugene, OR: Wipf & Stock, 1990), p. 169.

2. Hick, p. 176.

3. William James, *The Varieties of Religious Experience* (Lexington, KY: Renaissance Classics, 2012), p. 329.

4. Yoram Hazony, "An Imperfect God," *New York Times*, November 25, 2012, https://opinionator.blogs.nytimes.com/2012/11/25/an-imperfect -god/?_r=0. Cf. Yoram Hazony, *The Philosophy of Hebrew Scriptures* (Cambridge: Cambridge University Press, 2012).

5. John D. Caputo, *Hoping Against Hope: Confessions of a Postmodern Pilgrim* (Minneapolis: Fortress Press, 2015), p. 122.

6. David Hume, *Dialogues Concerning Natural Religion* (Indianapolis: Hackett, 1998), Part V, p. 37.

4. RELIGIOUS FICTIONALISM

Some material in this chapter was drawn from "How to Live a Lie," *The Stone* (blog), *New York Times*, November 2, 2015.

1. Karl Marx, *Early Writings* (New York: McGraw-Hill, 1963), p. 43.

2. For discussion of true myths, see Philip Kitcher, *Life after Faith: The Case for Secular Humanism* (New Haven: Yale University Press, 2014), pp. 73, 76–78, 81–82, 88, 92–93.

3. Jean Kazez, "Religious Fictionalism," blog post, April 24, 2011, http://kazez.blogspot.com/2011/04/religious-fictionalism.html.

4. Tamar Szabó Gendler, "Alief and Belief," *Journal of Philosophy* 105 (2008), pp. 634–63.

5. John D. Caputo, *Hoping Against Hope: Confessions of a Postmodern Pilgrim* (Minneapolis: Fortress Press, 2015), pp. 39, 61, 72.

6. Caputo, p. 118.

7. Caputo, p. 50.

8. Caputo, p. 115.

9. Caputo, pp. 122, 119.

10. Jesse Bering, *The Belief Instinct: The Psychology of Souls, Destiny, and the Meaning of Life* (New York: W.W. Norton, 2011), p. 77.

11. Bering, pp. 46–47.

12. Bering, p. 75.

13. Simone de Beauvoir, *Adieux: A Farewell to Sartre*, trans. Patrick O'Brien (New York: Pantheon, 1984), p. 438. Cf. Bering, p. 47.

14. Jean-Paul Sartre, *The Words*, trans. Bernard Frechtman (New York: George Braziller, 1964), p. 253.

15. John H. Gillespie, "Sartre and the Death of God," *Sartre Studies International* 22 (2016), p. 54.

5. IS FAITH A GIFT?

1. Sam Harris, *The End of Faith: Religion, Terror, and the Future of Reason* (New York: Norton, 2004), p. 232.

2. Blaise Pascal, *Pensées*, trans. A. J. Krailsheimer (New York: Penguin, 1995), p. 127, section 423.

3. David Hume, *Of the Standard of Taste* (Birmingham: Birmingham Free Press, 2013), p. 15.

4. Wilfred Cantwell Smith, *Faith and Belief: The Difference Between Them* (Oxford: Oneworld Publications, 1998), p. 171.

5. Smith, p. 169.

6. Stephen Batchelor, *The Faith to Doubt: Glimpses of Buddhist Uncertainty* (Berkeley: Counterpoint, 2015), p. 15.

7. Smith, p. 101.

8. Tertullian, *De Carne Christi* V, 4. Translated by Peter Holmes as *On the Flesh of Christ* (Lexington, KY: CreateSpace, 2017).

9. Miguel de Unamuno, *Tragic Sense of Life*, trans. J. E. Crawford Fitch (New York: Dover, 1954), p. 193.

10. Søren Kierkegaard, *Concluding Unscientific Postscript to Philosophical Fragments*, Vol. 1, trans. Howard V. Hong and Edna H. Hong (Princeton: Princeton University Press, 1992), p. 201.

11. Smith, p. 168.

12. Smith, p. 160.

13. Smith, p. 160.

14. Smith, p. 160.

15. Smith, p. 161.

16. Smith, p. 142.

17. Francis Spufford, *Unapologetic: Why, Despite Everything, Christianity Can Still Make Surprising Emotional Sense* (London: Faber and Faber, 2013), p. 68. Cf. Tim Crane, *The Meaning of Belief: Religion from an Atheist's Point of View* (Cambridge: Harvard University Press, 2017), p. 75.

18. Thomas Merton, *New Seeds of Contemplation* (New York: New Directions Books, 2007), p. 105.

19. Crane, p. 77.

20. Unamuno, p. 111.

21. Unamuno, p. 119.

22. Unamuno, p. 116.

23. Augustine, *Tractates on the Gospel of John 28–34, Fathers of the Church*, Vol. 88, trans. John W. Rettig (Washington, DC: Catholic University Press, 1993), p. 18.

24. *Catechism of the Catholic Church*, Section 159, www.vatican.va/archive/ccc_css/archive/catechism/p1s1c3a1.htm.

25. Jean-Luc Marion, *Believing in Order to See*, trans. Christina M. Gschwandtner (New York: Fordham University Press, 2017), p. xiv.

26. Marion, pp. 137–38.

27. Marion, p. 142.

28. Søren Kierkegaard, *Fear and Trembling/Repetition*, trans. Howard V. Hong and Edna H. Hong (Princeton: Princeton University Press, 1983), p. 53.

29. Friedrich Nietzsche, *The Antichrist* in *Twilight of the Idols/The Anti-Christ*, trans. R. J. Hollingdale (New York: Penguin, 1990), p. 181, section 52.

30. Walter Kaufmann, *From Shakespeare to Existentialism* (Garden City, NY: Anchor Books, 1960), p. 178.

31. Jerry A. Coyne, *Faith versus Fact: Why Science and Religion Are Incompatible* (New York: Penguin Books, 2015), p. xi.

32. Smith, p. 133.

33. Richard Beck, *The Authenticity of Faith: Varieties and Illusions of Religious Experience* (Abilene, TX: Abilene Christian University Press, 2012), p. 264.

34. Harris, p. 65.

35. Abraham Joshua Heschel, *God in Search of Man: A Philosophy of Judaism* (New York: Farrar, Straus and Giroux, 1955), pp. 35–36. Cf. Beck, p. 24.

36. Beck, p. 163.

37. Beck, p. 129.

38. Alvin Plantinga, *Warranted Christian Belief* (New York: Oxford University Press, 2000), p. 214.

39. Carl Sagan, *The Demon-Haunted World: Science as a Candle in the Dark* (New York: Random House, 1996), p. 173.

40. For more on the Flying Spaghetti Monster, see http://spaghettimonster .com. A similar unfalsifiable example was offered by the philosopher Bertrand Russell in the form of an undetectable teapot between Earth and Mars. See http://russellsteapot.net.

41. Ker Than, "Is the Abominable Snowman a Bear?" *National Geographic*, October 22, 2013, http://news.nationalgeographic.com/news/2013/10/131021 -yeti-abominable-snowman-bigfoot-polar-bear-cryptozoology.

42. Coyne, p. 119.

43. Coyne, p. 202.

6. A CIVIL DISCOURSE

1. Richard Feynman, "Cargo Cult Science," Caltech commencement address, Pasadena, CA, June 14, 1974, http://calteches.library.caltech.edu/51/2 /CargoCult.pdf.

2. Tim Crane, *The Meaning of Belief: Religion from an Atheist's Point of View* (Cambridge: Harvard University Press, 2017), pp. 179–80.

3. John Stuart Mill, *On Liberty* (New York: Penguin, 1985), p. 98.

4. Mill, p. 97.

5. Mill, p. 99.

6. Bryan Caplan, "The Ideological Turing Test," *EconLog* (blog), June 20, 2011, http://econlog.econlib.org/archives/2011/06/the_ideological.html.

7. George Lakoff and Mark Johnson, *Metaphors We Live By* (Chicago: University of Chicago Press, 1980), pp. 4–5.

8. It is one of the seven habits in Stephen R. Covey's *The 7 Habits of Highly Effective People* (New York: Simon and Schuster, 1989).

9. It is not clear if Wilde actually said this, but the point remains the same. And please forgive the sexism of the term "gentleman"—the point applies just as much to women as to men.

7. THE PHYSICIST'S HORSESHOE AND
THE ATHEIST'S PRAYER

Some material in this chapter was drawn from "Liberation through Compassion and Kindness: The Buddhist Eightfold Path as a Philosophy of Life," *Journal of Philosophy of Life* 3 (2013): 68–82.

1. This chapter speaks directly to the atheist. For the agnostic it can make perfect sense to pray. The agnostic's prayer is a bit like the act of watering a dead plant. One doesn't know if the plant will respond, but it seems worth a try. Anthony Kenny says, "There is no reason why someone who is in doubt about the existence of God should not pray for help and guidance on this topic as in other matters. Some find something comic in the idea of an agnostic praying to a God whose existence he doubts. It is surely no more unreasonable than the act of a man adrift in the ocean, trapped in a cave, or stranded on a mountainside, who cries for help though he may never be heard or fires a signal which may never be seen." *The God of the Philosophers* (Oxford: Oxford University Press, 1979), p. 129.

2. Along similar lines, Søren Kierkegaard says, "The prayer does not change God, but it changes the one who prays." *Upbuilding Discourses in Various Spirits*, ed. and trans. Howard V. Hong and Edna H. Hong (Princeton: Princeton University Press, 1993), p. 22.

3. From an atheist perspective, Ronald Aronson says, "Hope is simply and fundamentally the energy to keep on." *Living without God: New Directions for Atheists, Agnostics, Secularists, and the Undecided* (Berkeley: Counterpoint, 2008), p. 188.

4. David Kyle Johnson, *The Myths That Stole Christmas: Seven Misconceptions That Hijacked the Holiday (and How We Can Take It Back)* (Washington, DC: Humanist Press, 2015).

5. Liz Todd, "Why I Celebrate Christmas, by the World's Most Famous Atheist," *Daily Mail Online*, December 23, 2008, www.dailymail.co.uk/debate/article-1100842/Why-I-celebrate-Christmas-worlds-famous-atheist.html.

6. R. Elisabeth Cornwell, "A Very Atheist Christmas," https://richarddawkins.net/2012/12/a-very-atheist-christmas (originally published in the *Washington Post*, December 21, 2011).

7. James Kingsland, *Siddhartha's Brain* (New York: William Morrow, 2016), pp. 48, 60.

8. For example, J. Brewer et al., "Meditation Experience Is Associated with Differences in Default Mode Network Activity and Connectivity," *Proceedings of the National Academy of Sciences* 108 (2011), pp. 20254–59.

9. Sam Harris, *Waking Up: A Guide to Spirituality without Religion* (New York: Simon & Schuster, 2014).

10. Miguel de Unamuno wrote a poem, "The Atheist's Prayer":

> Hear my plea you, God who doesn't exist,
> and in your nonexistence gather these, my grumblings.
> You who never leave poor humans
> without false comfort. You don't resist
> our pleas and you disguise our desires.
> The more you move yourself away from my mind,
> the more I remember the calm fairy tales
> my nursemaid told me to sweeten sad nights.
>
> How vast you are, my God! You are so vast
> that you are nothing but an Idea; reality is so narrow
> however much it expands itself
>
> to meet you. I suffer at your cost,
> nonexistent God. For if you did exist
> I too would truly exist.

11. For a different, postmodern take on payer, see John D. Caputo, *Hoping Against Hope: Confessions of a Postmodern Pilgrim* (Minneapolis: Fortress Press, 2015), pp. 190–97.

12. See Aronson, pp. 42–64. Aronson says, "Prayer is not necessary, but gratitude is" (p. 64).

13. Richard Dawkins, *Unweaving the Rainbow* (Boston: Mariner, 2000), p. 1.

14. Michael Puett and Christine Gross-Loh, *The Path: What Chinese Philosophers Can Teach Us about the Good Life* (New York: Simon & Schuster, 2016), pp. 35–36.

15. Herbert Benson et al., "Study of the Therapeutic Effects of Intercessory Prayer (STEP) in Cardiac Bypass Patients: A Multicenter Randomized Trial of Uncertainty and Certainty of Receiving Intercessory Prayer," *American Heart Journal* 151 (2006), pp. 934–42.

16. Matthew Hutson, *The 7 Laws of Magical Thinking: How Irrational Beliefs Keep Us Happy, Healthy, and Sane* (New York: Penguin, 2013), p. 81.

17. See the classic example of climbing a mountain and needing to believe that you can make the leap you need to in William James, *The Will to Believe* (New York: Dover, 1956), p. 59.

18. Hutson, p. 102.

8. A SKEPTIC'S GUIDE TO RELIGIONS, SPIRITUAL AND SECULAR

1. The concept of family resemblance was introduced by Ludwig Wittgenstein, *Philosophical Investigations* (New York: Macmillan, 1953), pp. 65 ff.

2. The Amish have a practice in this spirit called Rumspringa. See http://groups.etown.edu/amishstudies/cultural-practices/rumspringa.

3. David Foster Wallace, "This Is Water," Kenyon College commencement address, Gambier, OH, May 21, 2005, http://web.ics.purdue.edu/~drkelly/DFWKenyonAddress2005.pdf.

4. See Jonathan Haidt, *The Righteous Mind: Why Good People Are Divided by Politics and Religion* (New York: Vintage, 2013), pp. 219–20.

5. Raymond Aron, *The Opium of the Intellectuals* (New Brunswick, NJ: Transaction Publishers, 2001).

6. Karl Marx, *Early Writings* (New York: McGraw-Hill, 1963), p. 43.

7. On the role that religions play in providing community, see Alain de Botton, *Religion for Atheists: A Non-Believer's Guide to the Uses of Religion* (New York: Vintage International, 2013), pp. 23–66.

8. On the paucity of secular alternatives, see Robert D. Putnam, *Bowling Alone: The Collapse and Revival of American Community* (New York: Touchstone Books, 2001).

9. John D. Caputo relates the story of a friend who remained in the priesthood despite being a lapsed Catholic. *Hoping Against Hope: Confessions of a Postmodern Pilgrim* (Minneapolis: Fortress Press, 2015), pp. 56–57.

INDEX